WORD WATCHER'S HANDBOOK

WORD WATCHER'S HANDBOOK

A Deletionary of the Most Abused and Misused Words

Phyllis Martin, friends, and many readers of the first edition

ST. MARTIN'S PRESS
New York

Library of Congress Cataloging in Publication Data

Martin, Phyllis Rodgers.
Word watcher's handbook.

1. English language—Idioms, corrections, errors.
I. Title.
PE1460.M29 1982   428.1   81-21526
ISBN 0-312-88937-2   AACR2
ISBN 0-312-88938-0 (pbk.)

Design by *Dennis J. Grastorf*

10 9 8 7 6 5 4 3 2 1

SECOND EDITION

The material for "Reviewing Foreign Menu Terms" is reprinted with permission from *Executive Etiquette,* copyright © 1979 by Marjabelle Young Stewart and Marian G. Faux. St. Martin's Press, New York.

The French pronunciation key is reprinted with permission from the *Larousse English/French: French/English Modern Dictionary,* copyright © Librairie Larousse, 1960, Librairie Larousse, Paris.

To Bruce, again

CONTENTS

ACKNOWLEDGMENTS

First, to Ann Landers. It is a joy to call her friend although we've never met. The Eppie Lederer who lives inside Ann Landers is an incredibly thoughtful person; hearing either of her names makes me glow with appreciation for her encouragement and caring.

To William Safire for citing me in his *On Language* column on two glorious occasions and then for allowing me to use his words in this book.

To Marjabelle Young Stewart and Marian Faux for graciously allowing me to include pertinent material from their book, *Executive Etiquette*. To Kermit Hummel for his help in adding the French pronunciations to this material.

To Bob Braun for his enthusiasm for my Deletionary. Bob continued to promote the book even after it was out of print. His awesome gift for selling to his viewers a product in which he believes helped to force this second edition.

To Barbara Anderson, my editor at St. Martin's Press. I once mistakenly typed "St. Barbara" when I addressed a letter to her. I erased the saint and started over. Next time, no erasure. I begin to perceive a halo around the head of my agent, too. Thanks, Emilie Jacobson.

Thanks also to my husband Bruce and my daughter Shirlie, for editorial help; to son Kipp, for his clipping service; to son Jay, for his list; to my sister Carolyn Carter; and to all those cousins who are a part of the "Cousins' Crusade."

And to Karen Blair, Agnes Rahman, Dr. Morleen Rouse, Bernard

Hoffman, Ruth Van Gelder, Dr. William McGrane, Gloria Exler, Fred Bennignus, Vada Stanley, Merlin James, Edna Halcomb, Carol Ray, Richard MacFarlane, Mary Pascal, and Karen Wiggins.

FOREWORD

This is a book about words. It evolved from a "word clinic" I give for just about any group that asks me. Since I am much better at talking about words than writing about them, I am tempted to ask you to read this book aloud. At least let me ask you to think about it as an oral communication that has been set in print in order to reach more people.

I chose the title, *Word Watcher's Handbook: A Deletionary of the Most Abused and Misused Words,* to show that the book is a way to acquire a trim vocabulary. By trim I do not mean one that is skinny but one that is in good condition; the words in the Deletionary are fat that should be eliminated. Other sections provide exercise for coordination and tone.

My goal is lofty:

To save the job seeker from a possible turndown.
To improve the job holder's chances for promotion.
To inspire the student to master the most important tool he or she will ever use: language.
To help everyone to avoid embarrassing mistakes in everyday conversation.

My ultimate aim is to help every reader delete conversational cholesterol that clogs lines of communication.

A college graduate should manage to lose a minimum of five words. A high-school graduate should manage to lose ten to twenty unwanted words. Younger students and dropouts can lose up to fifty in the first week.

INTRODUCTION

In his performance appraisal interview, Wallace B. said to his manager, "Let me *ax* you just one question."

The manager winced when he heard the word **ask** pronounced *ax*. It was all he could do to refrain from clenching his fist as he pretended not to have heard. In order to be fair, he asked Wallace to repeat what he'd just said. Indeed, it was *ax*.

Up to that point Wallace had been under consideration for an important promotion. The interview continued for some time but it was actually over the moment the one word—*ax*—was used.

Dave shouted, *"Irregardless* of what you say, I'm going to get a *pitcher* of you."

Dave's camera clicked but he didn't. For Sue ran across the lawn in the opposite direction. When a friend asked if Dave's approach had been too strong, Sue said yes and his language too weak.

How many times have you heard errors like these, as jarring to the ear as static on a radio? You are more aware of the error than of the content of what has just been said. Worst of all, the speaker has no idea that he has made a mistake.

Or perhaps you have heard a word pronounced differently

from the way you always thought it was pronounced, and thought, I wonder if I've been saying that right? You intend to look it up but somehow never do.

Even if you are a fairly well-read person with a reasonably good vocabulary, there may be just a few errors you are making that are as painful to some people as the errors above are to you. As you begin to read through this book, you are likely to be surprised at the number of errors that have slipped into your everyday speech.

The first three chapters of *Word Watcher's Handbook* are designed to attack a specific category of language misuse. The first chapter, "Deletionary," lists words you should remove from your vocabulary, either because they are hackneyed and trite (and may leave a similar impression of you) or because they simply are not words. The worst offenders are harmful to the health of your vocabulary. They're poison—throw them away forever. The second part of the Deletionary is a list of feeble phrases that may have been original at one time but have long since lost their punch.

Chapter 2, "Usage," contains words that are frequently misused. Included in this chapter is the section Unmatched Pairs, which lists pairs of words that sound alike or are frequently confused, with short explanations of which one to use when.

Chapter 3, "Pronunciation Pitfalls," is a selection of commonly mispronounced words and an easy-to-read guide to the correct way to say them.

The last three chapters of the book were added at the request of word clinic participants and readers of the first edition.

Here is the foolproof method for making sure the boners in this book will never appear in your speech:

As you go through the book, make a flash card for each word you were wrong about or unsure of, following the illustrations on pages 7–9. It may seem like busy work, as you measure and snip the cards and carefully print the words, but do it. You will be rewarded later by the convenience.

You will also be more likely to discipline yourself to study words that trouble you—once through the flash cards each day and you're finished. Put those cards out in plain view on your night stand or desk, where they will remind you of their existence. Remember, the task will get shorter each day as you throw away the cards you no longer need.

If you become bored with the flash-card method and like to fool around with tape recorders, try this method for variety: Make a recording of the words you would like to learn, leaving a gap of about five seconds after each word. If it is meaning you are trying to remember, pronounce the word correctly on the tape and give yourself enough time to write down the meaning on a blank sheet of paper before going on. Then compare your paper with the book and grade yourself. If you are working on pronunciation, say into the microphone, "How do you pronounce c-h-a-s-m?" You can write down the correct pronunciations.

You can also simply make a tape of the words that you have trouble pronouncing. Just hearing them over and over again while you wash the dishes or get dressed can help to impress them in your memory. It's best not to record any wrong pronunciations, even for test purposes, because hearing the word mispronounced will hamper your ear training.

Now for a few final touches that will improve your communication with others. Even perfect speech will not be effective unless you keep the listener in mind in the following ways:

- Beware of the sheer length of some words. They are tiring to a listener's ears. If it's clarity of communication that you seek, try plain, sturdy, sure-footed words; then, if you can't resist a long word, your listener will have the strength to absorb it.
- Don't make bounding leaps in your speech, leaving out the essential intermediate steps—or, even worse, filling in with "you knows," "uhms," and "et ceteras." Be articulate; the

listener needs to be carefully led. If you can't express what you mean clearly, imagine how fuzzy the listener's picture will be.

- To keep an audience's attention, make sure your speech is full of visual images. Examples are an excellent means of creating pictures.
- Learn to improve the pitch and volume of your own voice. Listen to yourself on a tape recorder, at least, and take a few voice-training lessons if you think you need them. You can be taught to lower the pitch of your voice, for instance.
- Use your dictionary as those hard-working lexicographers intended. Know that the job of the lexicographer is to *Report Usage,* not to arbitrate usage. The fact that you see a word in a dictionary does not mean the writers of the dictionary sanction the word in question. That is why many dictionaries contain special "correct usage" or "common error" sections.
- Read, but be careful about trying out new words before you are sure of their pronunciation.
- Go to a lecture now and then instead of a movie.
- Listen to a talk show on the radio, or watch one on television, instead of a situation comedy.
- Remember your normal share of the speaking time is only 50 percent in a conversation with one other person. It is proportionately less with a larger group. Exceed that share only when you are sure others agree you should.
- Finally, don't allow all these dos and don'ts to ruin brisk, original, pleasant speech. Be spontaneous and say things your way.

LISTENING

A large part of communicating well is listening well. Listen closely to the others instead of concentrating on what you're going to say next; then what you do say will make more sense. The most polished speech will sound foolish if you are not following the thread of the conversation.

Even more important, when you take the time to hear and

understand what the other person is really saying, you save marriages, friendships, and jobs and you learn the true art of communication.

Answer the following questions about yourself, and look back at them after a few weeks to see if you are improving your listening skills.

Are you a positive listener?

Do you say to the speaker, "Tell me about it"?

Do you give encouragement to the speaker and reassure him from time to time that you are with him?

Do you look at the speaker?

Do you follow the speaker's ideas a little further, asking specific questions and trying to hit on what the speaker's deepest interest in the subject is?

Do you listen for clues to what the speaker's interests are and search for an area of mutual interest?

Do you echo important messages, to make sure you understood them?

Are you a negative listener?

Do you say to the speaker, "I know just what you're going to say"?

Do you say, "We've tried that before" as soon as he begins an explanation, or, just as bad, when he's finished?

Do you look away from the speaker?

Do you think you know someone else's point of view before he tells you?

Do you decide in advance that you know more about the subject than the speaker does?

Do you decide ahead of time that the subject is dull? That the speaker is dull?

Do you find the merest pretext to turn the conversation back to yourself, your preoccupations, or your ideas?

A special note about the written word:
Commerce Secretary Malcolm Baldridge has a dandy idea

for eliminating irritating words from letters, speeches, and manuscripts.

The electronic word processors in his office are set up so that if an employee punches in one of forty-three forbidden words or phrases, a warning is flashed.

DON'T USE THAT WORD.

Many of the words on the Secretary's list are in this book because they annoy other people, too. Some of the forbidden words are **viable**, **interface**, **prioritize** and **needless to say**.

So, why not make a list of terms your boss, your editor, or your friends don't like or that you misuse and feed them into your word processor?

Finally, a word of advice that has nothing to do with speaking or listening: Kind words are more important than the kind of words you use.

SAMPLE FLASH CARDS

You can use different colors of paper for deletions, definitions, and pronunciations.

Deletionary

I must delete the phrase
can't hardly
from my vocabulary

Front

The correct phrase is
can hardly

Back

Usage

The word
suspicion
is a noun. You have a
suspicion; you suspect.

Front

Do not say,
I suspicion;
say I **suspect**.

Back

Pronunciation

The correct pronunciation
of **nuclear**
is _____

Front

noo·klee·ur.
Do not insert a **U**
after the **C** in
nuclear.

Back

1

DELETIONARY

When you use too many words, you tire your listener and make it more difficult for him to hear the important words. You can also give the impression that you are fond of the sound of your own voice, when in truth you are just speaking as you are used to speaking, with all the bad habits you have picked up along the way. This chapter will guide you in clearing away the excess words and phrases that are cluttering your speech. It will help to make you into one of those admirable people of whom it is said, "He spoke a few well-chosen words."

Some of the words in the Deletionary are just plain wrong and make a far worse impression of you than verbosity does. If the nonwords that follow have crept into your speech, make that flash card now and be sure that when the card is finally thrown away, the nonword is gone forever, too.

The list includes trite and overused expressions as well as wordy and wrong ones. Notice that although old clichés are dreary, there is nothing more warmed-over-sounding than yesterday's slang.

absolutely	Don't use this word when you mean *yes*.
accidently	You mean **accidentally**. Pronounce all five syllables: **ak•si•den•tahl•lee**.
acrost, acrossed	The word you want is **across**.

advance planning	What other kind of planning is there? The same goes for *advance warning*.
afeared	This is a corruption of the word **afraid**. Please delete it from your vocabulary.
ahold	Not standard English. Drop the a.
ain't	Colloquial. **Is not** and **are not** are preferable.
things being equal	What could this possibly mean, when you think about it?
alot	Do not make one word from two. It is **a lot**.
and stuff	A filler phrase, to make your statement sound more complete than it is.
and that	Same as *and stuff*.
anyways	Say **anyway**.
anywheres	No **s** here either; it's **anywhere**.
aren't I	When you use this phrase, you are contracting the words *are I not*. **Am I not** is preferred to *aren't I*.
ascared	Not standard English. The words are **scared** and **afraid**.
as you know	If they know, you shouldn't be telling them again. **As you may know** makes more sense, but don't use it just to be polite.
at this point in time	One of the many verbose phrases that should be replaced by good old **now**.
whole nother thing	The word **another** is divided and **whole** is stuck inside. Say instead, **That's another matter entirely**.
balance	Don't use this word as a substitute for **rest**, although you may use it when speaking of money: **The balance is due when we pick up the chair**.
basket case	Not a nice expression, especially if it's used for what it means.

beautiful! Appropriate about once a year.

beautiful person Doesn't this phrase imply that everyone else isn't beautiful? *Beautiful person* is passé now, and it's about time. The simple **I like him** has more force than *He's a beautiful person.*

be that as it may Archaic and pedantic-sounding. The word **but** will do.

blame it on You can **blame** a person, or **put the blame on** him.

boughten A nonword. Use **bought**.

bretzel You mean **pretzel**; and it starts with **p**.

bust Avoid saying *bust* when you mean **burst**.

can Don't use as a substitute for **may**. **Can** denotes ability; **may** denotes permission.

can't hardly This is a double negative and should not be used. Say **can hardly**.

case Don't use as a substitute for **instance** or **example**. *In most cases* should be **In most instances**.

character Slang when used to mean a "unique personality."

charisma Once a lovely word meaning "a special gift of the Holy Spirit," **charisma** is now applied to everyone from politicians to underground movie stars.

chauvinist How about saying, for example, **He's condescending to women?** It's more specific, less rhetorical.

cold slaw It is **cole slaw.**

complected The word is **complexioned.**

confrontation Sometimes **meeting** will do.

consciousness raising Overused. How about "deepening awareness" for the sake of variety?

consensus of opinion The idea of *opinion* is built into the word **consensus.**

continue on	Redundant. Just say **continue.**
cool	An overworked fad word from the fifties.
curiously enough	Say **curiously.** It's more effective.
disadvantaged	A euphemism for **poor.**
drapes	It's **draperies**.
drownded	The past tense of **drown** is **drowned.**
due to the fact that	Just say **because.** By the way, only a thing can be **due** to another thing. You cannot say, for instance, *We capsized, due to the heavy wind;* you must say **because of.**
emote	Not a word. To **show emotion** is the equivalent, or you may be more precise.
encounter	**Meet?**
enthused	Not a word. Say **enthusiastic.**
equally as	Redundant. Just say **equally.**
escalate	There's nothing wrong with this new word, except that it's overused.
estimated at about	Delete the *about:* that's part of the meaning of **estimate.**
et	Not a word. Say **we have eaten** or **we ate**— never *we et.*
evacuate	To make empty. For example, **The building was evacuated** (not *the tenants were evacuated).*
excape	The word you want is **escape.** There is no **x** in the word.
expertise	Use **knowledge** or **experience** for a change.
famed	A self-conscious coinage by the mass media, as if to say, "He's famed, and *we* famed him." **Famous** is still preferred.
fantastic	Overworked. Try **fanciful, odd, grotesque.** When it is used to express vague positive feelings, it is sadly misused.
finalize	**Finish, complete, conclude?**
flustrated	A combination of **flustered** and **frus-**

	trated? Be precise, and use one or the other.
for free	**Free** or **for nothing** are fine, but *for free* sounds childish.
frame of reference	**Background?** **Viewpoint?** **Academic discipline?**
gent	Say **gentleman** or **man.**
gross	Overused. Try **vulgar** or **coarse.**
growth	To those who laud all *growth,* I say, "Remember cancer and kudzu." Use **increase in size** or **volume.**
guesstimate	Means "a very rough estimate"? Say so. *Guesstimate* may have been mildly amusing the first time it was used.
heartrendering	If you must use this tired expression, make it **heartrending.** You render fat, not hearts.
heighth	Not a word. The term you want is **height.** Pronounce it **hite** (rhymes with **kite**).
herewith	Herewith means "enclosed with this," so it is redundant to say *enclosed herewith.* Just say **Herewith is the package I promised you.**
hinderance	Though derived from the word **hinder,** this verb's noun form is **hindrance,** and it has only two syllables.
hisself	Not a word. The correct word is **himself.**
hopefully	Say **I hope** or even plain old **perhaps:** the hope is sometimes evident in the context.
how about that?	A tired old nonremark.
hunnert	The word you want is **hundred.**
I been	Say **I have been.**
I done	**I have done,** or **I did.**
I don't think	How can you express an opinion if you don't think? Try **I think not.** The phrase *I don't think* hurts many ears.

incidently	The word is **incidentally,** and it has five syllables.
in my opinion, I think	**I think** is sufficient. *In my personal opinion* is of the same order.
insightful	Overused. Try **discerning, intuitive, penetrating.**
irregardless	The word is **regardless.**
it don't	This is a contraction of *it do not,* an incorrect phrase. Say **it does not** or **it doesn't.**
learning experience	One either learns from experience or one doesn't; the phrase is meaningless.
love	If **like** will do, you're using the word **love** too loosely.
marginal	When used in phrases such as *a marginal difference,* the word means nothing that **small** doesn't mean. Unless you're referring to a margin, say **small.**
meaningful dialogue meaningful experience meaningful relationship	The word *meaningful* evokes a negative response in many people. I've had complaints about *meaningful* dialogue, *meaningful* experience and *meaningful* relationship.
muchly	Avoid. This word was all right in Shakespeare's time, but it is considered affected and incorrect today.
my personal opinion	If it's your opinion, then by definition it's personal.
needless to say	A filler. If it were needless, you wouldn't be saying it.
never before in the past	Pick one: **before** or **in the past.**
nowheres	The word is **nowhere** (without the **s**).
off of	Omit the *of.* **Get off the bus.**
okay?	When used intermittently in a narrative, this word annoys the listener by begging for his approval.

ongoing	Most sentences featuring *ongoing* are strengthened by omitting it.
orientate	Not standard English. Say **orient.**
oughta	Not standard English. Say **ought to** or **should.**
out loud	**Aloud** is preferred.
out of	Use with care. In some phrases the *of* is superfluous, as in *look out of the window* or *walk out of the door.* Unless you're a termite, make that **out the door.** You can only get out of something you have been in; i.e., you can **walk out of a building.**
overly	The prefix **over-** sounds better, or just say **too.**
over with	Omit the *with.*
personal friend	In most instances, **friend** is enough.
personally, I think	Same as *my personal opinion*—the *personally* is unnecessary.
plastic	Let's return this one to its dictionary meaning, and to all "plastic" parents: May your offspring think of something more original.
please?	If you're speaking German, you're allowed to say, *Bitte?* ("Please?"), meaning, "What did you say?" Since many people do not understand this colloquialism, in English it is better to avoid it. Then, too, there are many who understand it but can't stand it.
presently	If you mean "now," say **now.** You may use **presently** to mean "soon," but **soon** is shorter and less pretentious.
prior to	Say **before.**
quote	Correct as a verb (**He quoted Emerson. May I quote you?**) but not as a noun (say **a quotation from Emerson**).
rap	For "talk," a little shopworn.

really If you're using it for emphasis, rather than to mean "as opposed to appearances," eliminate it.

relatively **Relatively** can be nothing but an attempt to get yourself off the hook when you think you've said something too definite. If you can't say what's relative to what, chances are nothing is, and you should leave this word out. *Relatively speaking* almost always means nothing.

relevant The word *relevant* appears in this section because so many people complained that they are tired of hearing it. You may want to say **pertinent** or **to the point.**

reoccur The correct word is **recur.**

rewarding Try to name what the rewards are.

right on! Originally a political rallying cry, and now misused to express approval of what has just been said. This phrase is tired anyway and would best be marched right on out.

Sahara desert Sahara means "desert," so just say **the Sahara.** The same goes for *Rio Grande River* and *Mt. Fujiyama* (it's the **Rio Grande** and **Fujiyama,** or **Mt. Fuji**).

see what I mean? Another phrase, like *okay?*, that begs approval. Eliminate it from your vocabulary.

snuck Not standard English. Say **sneaked.**

spastic A word that is offensive except when correctly used as a medical term.

start off Just say **start.** You don't need *off* after it.

supposing The word is **suppose,** as in, **Suppose you go first.**

swang Dialectical past tense form of **swing. Swung** is preferred.

tell it like it is Old as old slang.

thanking you, I remain	Old and trite.
that fact is, is that	This phrase is wholly unnecessary, but the double **is** sounds tongue-tied besides.
theirselves	The word is **themselves.**
this here	If the object or person referred to is present, **this** alone is enough. If it's not present, substitute **a** for **this.** Say **A boy I met at the beach,** not *This boy I met at the beach.*
thusly	Say simply **thus.**
umble	The word is **humble.** Sound the **h.**
unbeknownst	Pompous substitute for **unknown.**
underprivileged	Say **poor** instead.
undoubtably	The word is **undoubtedly,** pronounced **un•doẃ•ted•lee.**
valid	A tired word. Try **cogent. Well-grounded. Solid. Genuine.**
viable	**Possible, capable of living, alive?**
widow woman	**Widow** is sufficient. The word already encompasses the idea of woman, just as **widower** includes the idea of man.
-wise	As a handy suffix, meaning "in any way whatsoever related to the root word," **-wise** is misused.
you can say that again	Conversational overkill. You can nod politely to show that you agree.
you know	A hedge for when the speaker doesn't know how to explain something. *You know* can get to be an annoying habit; better to eliminate it altogether.
youse	Please rid your vocabulary of this nonword. The plural of **you** is **you.**

RUNNERS-UP

Before we leave this section of the chapter, let me mention that almost everyone dislikes professional jargon, "trendy" words, and "buzz" words. Teachers complain about social workers, doctors about lawyers—you get the idea: Nobody wants to be on the outside of a discussion.

Take a look at this list of runners-up in the Most Overused Words contest. You don't have to delete these words from your vocabulary entirely, but check to see that you are not giving some of them more than their fair share of the air waves.

alienated
articulate (as a verb)
awesome
bizarre
climate (other than the weather variety)
concept
controversial
credibility
depersonalization
dialogue
dynamics
elegant
enrichment
exciting
expertise
holistic
impact (as a verb)
interface
involved
manic
obscene

operative
oppressed
overreact
paranoid
politicized
posture (for "attitude")
priorize, also prioritize
rationalize
rhetoric
rip-off
scenario
share
structure (as a verb)
substantive
superlative
thrust
traumatic
ventilate (feelings)
veritable
viable

FEEBLE-PHRASE FINDER

Many of the following phrases once evoked vivid images; some were downright poetic. But now they slip out automatically—"as a bee" following "busy" before we can stop ourselves. They evoke nothing in the listener except weariness.

You have a right to know how I compiled this list. And if

you're thinking, "My, doesn't she have her nerve?" I'll agree with you. It takes nerve. Especially since a few of my favorite expressions are included.

I believe I started this back in freshman English at the University of Cincinnati. And I know I used such a list for a secretarial program I led at the executive offices of Procter & Gamble. I know, too, that all of us in personnel agreed to help each other "banish the bromide."

Naturally, an updated version of that list became part of my current Word Watchers' Clinic. But the collection you see here has many contributors: readers of the first edition of *Word Watcher's Handbook,* my family, friends, teachers, business associates, and every person who has been part of the word clinic.

I don't stand at the podium spieling off what I think are hackneyed phrases. Participants tell me—on cards provided or by taking the floor and telling the class and me. They also tell me by phone. Or mail. And by sending word with those who sign for later sessions.

Only after many people have commented negatively on a trite expression does it "make the list." Each phrase you see had numerous nay votes.

Have a nice day wasn't even included in the first edition but it ran a close second to *You know* this time. Together they garnered more votes than all the other phrases combined. That's why they appear in a paragraph all by themselves.

These canned similes, platitudes, bromides, clichés, and old saws are long overdue for oblivion. Won't you give them the rest they deserve?

abreast of the times
absence makes the heart grow
  fonder
ace in the hole
accidents will happen
acid test
according to one's lights

add insult to injury
after all is said and done
age before beauty
a good time was had by all
all in all
all is not gold that glitters
all too soon

"Today I had 23 'Is it hot enough for yous,' 16 'Have a nice days,' four 'Don't call me—I'll call yous,' two 'How's the world treatin' yous,' and one 'Buzz off, Mac!'"

Reprinted by permission of the Chicago *Tribune*-New York *News* Syndicate, Inc.

all to the good
all walks of life
all wool and a yard wide
all work and no play
almighty dollar
along the line
also-ran
any and all
a pound of flesh
apple-pie order
arms of Morpheus
as a whole
as for me

asleep at the switch
as luck would have it
as the crow flies
at death's door
at first blush
at loose ends
at the crossroads
at this juncture
at wit's end
auspicious occasion
avoided like the plague
back to the drawing board
back to the wall

banker's hours
bark up the wrong tree
bated breath
bathed in tears
bat out of hell
battle for life/of life
beard the lion in his den
beat a dead horse
beat a hasty retreat
bee in her bonnet
beg to advise
believe you me
best bib and tucker
best-laid plans of mice and men
better late than never
better to have loved and lost
between a rock and a hard place
between the devil and the deep blue sea
between two stools
between you, me and the lamppost (fence post)
bird in the hand
bite off more than one can chew
bite the bullet
bite the dust
bitter end
black as coal
blanket of snow
blazing inferno
blood is thicker than water
blow hot and cold
blow off steam
blow your own horn
blow your top
blushing bride
bolt from the blue
bone of contention
bone to pick
born with a silver spoon

bosom of the family
bottom line
bottom of the barrel
brain trust
break the ice
break your neck
breathe a sigh of relief
bright and early
bright-eyed and bushy-tailed
bright future
bring home the bacon
bring to a head
bring up the rear
briny deep
brown as a berry
bucking the trend
budding genius
buffeted by fate
bull by the horns
bundle of nerves
burning question
burn the midnight oil
burn your bridges
bury the hatchet
busman's holiday
busy as a bee
butter-and-egg man
butterflies in the stomach
by hook or crook
by the same token
by the skin of the teeth
by the sweat of his brow
callow youth
calm before the storm
can of worms
can't fight City Hall
can't make head nor tail of
carry the ball
cart before the horse
cash on the barrel
cast bread upon the water

casting aspersions
cast the first stone
cast your lot with
cast your pearls before swine
caught red-handed
change your tune
checkered career
chip off the old block
clean as a whistle
clear as a bell
clear as crystal
clear as mud
clearing the decks
coals to Newcastle
cock-and-bull story
cold as ice
cold feet
cold sweat
come in out of the rain
come out in the wash
consensus of opinion (redundant as well as tiresome)
conspicuous by his absence
contents noted
cool as a cucumber
could care less
crack the whip
crash the gate
credibility gap
crooked as a dog's hind legs
crow to pick
crucial third-down situation
cry for the moon
cry over spilt milk
cry wolf
curiously enough (you don't need the enough)
cut the mustard
dead as a doornail
dead giveaway
deaf as a post

demon rum
depths of despair
devil to pay
diabolical plot
diamond in the rough
did a number
didn't know enough to come in out of the rain
didn't know from Adam
didn't lift a finger
die is cast
dirty old man
distance lends enchantment
distinguished speaker
don't put all your eggs in one basket
don't take any wooden nickels
doomed to disappointment
doting parent
down in the mouth
down my alley
draw the line
drink like a fish
drop in the bucket
drown his sorrow
drunk as a skunk
dull as dishwater (ditchwater)
dull thud
during the time that
dyed in the wool
each and every
eager beaver
early on
ear to the ground
easier said than done
eat, drink, and be merry
eat your hat
eleventh hour
enclosed please find
ends of the earth
everything went along nicely

exception proves the rule
explore every avenue
eyeball to eyeball
eyes bigger than one's stomach
eyes like saucers
eyes like stars
eyes of the world
face the music
fair and square
fair sex
far be it from me
far cry
fast and loose
fat's in the fire (a favorite of the
    late Erle Stanley Gardner—he
    could get by with it)
feather in his cap
feel his oats
feet of clay
few and far between
few well-chosen words
field of endeavor
fill the bill
filthy lucre
fine and dandy
finger in every pie
first and foremost
first pop out of the box
fish or cut bait
fish out of water
flash in the pan
flat as a pancake
flat on your back
flip your lid
flog a dead horse
fly-by-night
fly in the ointment
fly off the handle
fond farewell
fools rush in
foregone conclusion

foreseeable future
for my part
for the pure and simple reason
free as the air
fresh as a daisy
fresh out of
from rags to riches
frozen stiff
frying pan into the fire
gainfully employed (you don't
    need the gainfully)
gala occasion
game plans
garden variety
gentle as a baby
gentle as a lamb
get in one's hair
get it off your chest
get the sack
get to the point
get your dander up
gild the lily
gird your loins
give a piece of your mind
give a wide berth
give the devil his due
give short shrift to
give the gate
glad rags
go against the grain
God's country
go hat in hand
gone to seed
good as gold
good as new
go on the warpath
goose that laid the golden egg
go scot-free
go the whole hog
got his number
go to pieces

go to the dogs
got the upper hand
got up on the wrong side of the bed
grain of salt
graphic account
great hue and cry
greatness thrust upon
green as grass
green with envy
Grim Reaper
grin like a Cheshire cat
ground below (Since the ground is usually below, you probably don't need to say below.)
gum up the works
had the privilege
hail fellow well met
hair of the dog
hair's breadth
hair stand on end
halcyon days
hale and hearty
half a mind to
hammer and tongs
hand in glove
hand to mouth
handwriting on the wall
hang by a thread
hang in there, baby
happy as a lark
hard as nails
hard row to hoe
has a screw loose
has-been
HAVE A NICE DAY
have another think coming
haven't seen you in a coon's age
head above water
head and shoulders above
head over heels

heart in my mouth
heart in the right place
heart of gold
heart of hearts
hem and haw
herculean task
hide your light under a bushel
high-handed
high on the hog
hit below the belt
hit the nail on the head
hit the sack
hit your head against a stone wall
hold a candle to
hold the bag
hold the phone
hold your horses
hold your peace
holier than thou
hook, line, and sinker
hook or crook
hornet's nest
horns of a dilemma
horse of a different color
hungry as a bear
hurling invectives
I can't believe I ate the whole thing
if and when
if the shoe fits
if you follow me
ignorance is bliss
I'll buy that
I'll drink to that
in a pleasing manner
in a tight spot
in cahoots with
in conclusion would state
in full swing
in my judgment

in no uncertain terms
in one ear and out the other
in one fell swoop
in other words
in our midst (incorrect and mis-
    quoted—see Matthew 18:20)
inspiring sight
in spite of the fact that
institution of higher learning
interesting to note
intestinal fortitude
in the final analysis
in the know
in the last analysis
in the light of
in the long run
in the midst of
in the same boat
in this day and age
in touch with
irons in the fire
irony of fate
it depends on whose ox is being
    gored
it goes without saying
it's a whole new ball game
it stands to reason
Johnny-come-lately
Johnny-on-the-spot
joined together
join the club
jumping-off place
jump the gun
jump to conclusions
just bear with me
just to inform you
keep a stiff upper lip
keep body and soul together
keep the ball rolling
keep the pot boiling

keep your eye on the ball
keep your eyes peeled
kick in the teeth
kill the fatted calf
kill two birds with one stone
know the ropes
labor of love
lady of leisure
land-office business
last but not least
last straw
law unto herself
lead-pipe cinch
lean and hungry look
lean over backward
leap in the dark
leave in the lurch
leave no stone unturned
left-handed compliment
legend in his own time
let it all hang out
let's face it
let the cat out of the bag
let your hair down
level with me
lick into shape
light as a feather
like a bump on a log
like a lead balloon
limp as a rag
lips sealed
little did I think when
little old lady
lit up like a Christmas tree
live and let live
live high off the hog
live in hopes that
live it up
live off the fat of the land
loaded for bear

lock, stock, and barrel
long arm of the law
long time no see
look a gift horse in the mouth
lose your marbles
lose your shirt
lot of laughs
lucky stiff
lump in the throat
mad as a wet hen
make a clean breast of it
make a long story short/make a long story longer
make a mountain out of a molehill
make a pitch
make ends meet
make hay while the sun shines
make it perfectly clear
make no bones
make short work of
make the air blue
make the rounds (unless you're a doctor)
make things hum
master of all he surveys
may be favored
mean no offense
meets the eye
meets with your approval
method in his madness
might and main
mind your p's and q's
misery loves company
missed the boat
moment of truth
momentous decision
moot point
moot question
more easily said than done
more sinned against than sinning
more than meets the eye
more than she bargained for
more the merrier
motley crew
mute testimony
my bag
my door is always open
nagging headache
nail to the cross
naked truth
near at hand
near future
near miss
neat as a bandbox
necessary evil
neck and neck
neck of the woods
needle in a haystack
needless to say
needs no introduction
neither fish nor fowl
neither rhyme nor reason
never a dull moment
never in the history of
never too late
new broom sweeps clean
new lease on life
new wine in old bottles
nipped in the bud
nitty gritty
no expense has been spared
no great shakes
no leg to stand on
no man in his right mind
none the worse for wear
no place like home
no reflection on you, but
no respecter of persons

nose out of joint
nose to the grindstone
no skin off my nose
no strings attached
not a leg to stand on
not by a long shot
nothing succeeds like success
nothing to sneeze at
nothing ventured
not to be sneezed at
not to exceed
not wisely but too well
not worth a Continental
not worth the paper it's written
   on
no way
nth degree
number is up
of a high order
off the record
of the first order
of the first water
old as Methuselah
old as the hills
old before his time
old head on young shoulders
old stomping/stamping ground
on all fours
on bended knee
on cloud nine
one and only
one and the same
on Easy Street
one foot in the grave
on his last legs
on pins and needles
on the fence
on the level
on the mark
on the ragged edge

on the spot
on top of the world
opportunity knocks but once
other fish to fry
other side of the coin
ours is not to reason why
out in left field
out of sight, out of mind
out of sorts
out of the mouths of babes
out of the woods
over a barrel
over the hill
ox to the slaughter
package solutions
pain in the neck
painting the town
pale as a ghost
part and parcel
pass the buck
pass the time of day
pave the way for
pay the piper
peer group
penny for your thoughts
period of time
perish the thought
personal growth
pet peeve
Philadelphia lawyer
picture of health
piece of your mind
pillar of society
pillar to post
pinch hitter
pin it on her/him
pipe dream
plan your work and work your
   plan
play a waiting game

play both ends against the
  middle
play fast and loose
play into the hands of
play it by ear
play to the grandstand
play up to
play with fire
play your cards right
point with pride
poor as a church mouse
power corrupts
powers that be
present company excepted
pretty as a picture
pretty kettle of fish
primrose path
protests too much
pull chestnuts from the fire
pull the wool over his/her eyes
pull up stakes
pull your leg
pull your own weight
pull yourself together
pure and simple
pure as the driven snow
put a bug in his ear
put on the dog
put on your thinking cap
put our heads together
put that in your pipe and smoke
  it
put the bite on
putty in his/her hands
put up job
put your cards on the table
put your foot down
put your foot in it
put your foot in your mouth
put your hand to the plow

put your shoulder to the wheel
quick as a bunny
quick as a flash
quick as a wink
rack and ruin
rack your brain
raining cats and dogs
raise the dead
raise your sights
rake over the coals
ran circles around
rank has its privileges
rattle the wrong cage
read between the lines
read him/her like a book
read the riot act
really and truly
red as a beet
red-carpet treatment
rich as Croesus
rich beyond your wildest
  dreams
ride the gravy train
ride roughshod over
right man in the right place
right on the head
right up my alley
ring a bell
ring true
ripe old age
rise to the occasion
roaring success
rock of Gibraltar
roll out the red carpet
room at the top
rose-colored glasses
rough and ready
rough and tumble
round of applause
rub the wrong way

run for your money
run-of-the-mill
run up a red flag
sacred cow
sad but true
sadder but wiser
sad to tell
sail under false colors
same the whole word over
same wave length
save for a rainy day
save your breath
save your own skin
sawdust trail
school of hard knocks
seal his doom
sea of faces
see a man about a dog
see beyond the nose on her face
seek his fortune
seek his own level
see my way clear
see the light of day
seething mass of humanity
self-made man
sell him a bill of goods
sell like hot cakes
senior citizens (this has some
  defenders)
set teeth on edge
set the world on fire
set up shop
set your cap for
set your heart upon
seventh heaven
shadow of a doubt
shadow of his/her former self
shake a leg
shake a stick at
shake in my boots

shape of things to come
share these thoughts/words
shed a little light on the subject
she's on cloud nine
ships that pass in the night
shoot the breeze
shoot the works
short and sweet
shot in the arm
shoulder to the wheel
sibling rivalry
sick and tired
sigh of relief
sight for sore eyes
sight to behold
sight unseen
sign of the times
silence is golden
silent as the grave
since time immemorial
single most
sing like a bird
sink or swim
sitting pretty
sixes and sevens
six of one and half dozen of the
  other
skate on thin ice
skin alive
skin and bones
skin deep
skirt around the edge of
slowly but surely
small world
smart money
smelled like a rose
snake in the grass
snowed under
sock it to me
soft as snow

soft shoulder to cry on
soft spot in his/her heart
so help me Hannah
some kind of
something else
something's rotten in Denmark
so sue me
sound the trumpets
sow wild oats
spanner in the works
split hairs
spread yourself too thin
square meal
square peg in a round hole
square your conscience
stand on your own two feet
stand your ground
start from scratch
staying power
steal a march
steal your thunder
stick around awhile
stick-in-the-mud
stick in your craw
stick to the ribs
stick to your guns
stick your neck out
stiff-necked
stiff upper lip
still waters run deep
stock in trade
straight and narrow
straight as an arrow
straight from the horse's mouth
straight from the shoulder
strange as it seems
strange but true
strangely enough (just strangely
  will do)
straw in the wind

street of dreams
strike it rich
strike while the iron is hot
strike your fancy
string along with
strong as an ox
struck dumb
stubborn as a mule
stuff and nonsense
stuffed shirt
subsequent to
sum and substance
sumptuous repast
sun-drenched
supreme sacrifice
sweeten the kitty
swing a deal
tables are turned
take a back seat
take a leaf out of one's book
take a shine to
take it easy
take it lying down
take stock in
take the liberty
take to his heels
take words out of his mouth
talk through your hat
telling blow
tell it to the Marines
tell tales out of school
tender mercies
that is to say
that's it in a nutshell
the best-laid plans
the foreseeable future
theirs not to reason why
the proud possessor
there's a method in his madness
the very nature of things

the wheels of the gods grind slowly
the whole ball of wax
thick as thieves
thick-skinned
thin as a rail
think tank
thin-skinned
this side of the grave
those with whom we come in contact
through thick and thin
throw a wrench in the machinery
throw in the sponge
throw in the towel
throw the book at
tidy sum
time hangs heavy
time immemorial
time is of the essence
time was ripe
tiny tots
tired as a dog
tired but happy
tit for tat
to all intents and purposes
toe the mark
to gird up one's loins
to make a long story short
tongue in cheek
too funny for words
too many irons in the fire
too numerous to mention
tooth and nail
top drawer
to play ball with
to string along
to tell the truth
to the bitter end

to the manner born
touch with a ten-foot pole
tough act to follow
tough as nails
tower of strength
tread lightly
trials and tribulations
trip the light fantastic
true blue
true facts (facts are true)
try men's souls
truth to tell
turnabout is fair play
turn a cold shoulder
turn a deaf ear
turn a hand
turn back the clock
turn over a new leaf
turn the other cheek
turn the tables
turn thumbs down
turn up your nose
two strings to your bow
ugly as sin
ugly duckling
unable to see the forest for the trees
undercurrent of excitement
under the wire
uneasy truce
unless and until
untiring efforts
up against it
ups and downs
value system
vast concourse
view with alarm
virtual standstill
viselike grip
wait on hand and foot

walk a tightrope
walks of life
warm as toast
warm the cockles of one's heart
wash one's dirty linen in public
wash one's hands of it
water under the bridge
water over the dam
way out
way to go
weaker sex
wear and tear
weather eye open
wee small hours
wended their way
whipping boy
white as a sheet
wide of the mark
wide open spaces
wild oats
wind out of your sails
win your spurs
wishy-washy
with a high hand

with all my heart
with a vengeance
with bated breath
with might and main
without a doubt
without a prayer
without rhyme or reason
wolf from the door
wolf in sheep's clothing
wonderful world of—
word to the wise
world is his oyster
worse for wear
worthy opponent
would I lie to you?
wreathed in smiles
wrong end of the stick
yellow-bellied
YOU KNOW
you'd better believe it
your guess is as good as mine
your kind indulgence
you've come a long way, baby

2

USAGE

Once you have removed the static from your communications system by eliminating all the words that are wrong, you can then improve your image even further by following these two rules:

1. *Don't be afraid to use the correct word. It may sound a little stilted to you, or strange, but most of the strangeness is due to the fact that you haven't used the word before. Or if you have, you haven't used it correctly. Don't avoid the word; learn its meaning and then use it.*
2. *Never talk down to those around you by using errors in your own speech.*

<table>
<tr>
<td>aggravate</td>
<td>"To make worse, to increase," as in to aggravate a condition. Do not use when you mean irritate or annoy. I am irritated rather than I am aggravated.</td>
</tr>
<tr>
<td>agree to, agree with</td>
<td>You agree to a plan or suggestion and agree with a person. One thing agrees with another thing.</td>
</tr>
<tr>
<td>almost</td>
<td>"Not quite." Do not say most for almost. Almost everybody was there.</td>
</tr>
<tr>
<td>alternative</td>
<td>Some careful speakers and writers insist that there can be only two alternatives in any situation. If there are more, they become choices or possibilities. Some say</td>
</tr>
</table>

that if you *have* to choose one of them, they are **alternatives**, no matter how many there are.

among Use **among** when referring to three or more items. Use **between** if there are only two. **Between you and me. Among the three of us.** In very rare instances, **between** may be proper with more than two, as when the action described can only take place between two of the several at one time.

amount Use **amount** to refer to a general quantity. **There was a large amount of work to be done.** Use **number** to refer to items that can be counted.

and Do not use this word when you mean **to**; for example, **come to see me**, not *come and see me*. See TRY AND.

angry One is angry **at** a situation but angry **with** a person.

anxious "To be worried, apprehensive." Do not confuse with **eager**, wanting something very much.

anyplace Careful speakers and writers avoid this term as a substitute for **anywhere**. In sentences such as **We couldn't find any place to park**, it is two words.

as "Equally, in the same manner." **As** is correct before a phrase. **She thinks as I do.** Do not substitute *like*, which is used before nouns or pronouns. See LIKE.

at This word should not be used at the end of a sentence starting with **where**. Say **Where is the book?** not *Where is the book at?*

author This is a noun, not a verb. Instead of saying *She authored the book*, say **She is the author of the book**.

balance Used in accounting or to describe a state

of equilibrium. When your meaning is "the rest of," use **remainder**. When speaking of money, you may say **The balance is due when we pick up the chair**.

barely Guard against using with other negative words, as **barely** is already negative, and two negatives cancel each other. Say **can barely**, not *can't barely*.

basis Remember that the plural form is **bases**, pronounced **bay'•seez**.

beside "At the side of, alongside." Do not use *of* after it. **The chair is beside the desk**. Compare with BESIDES.

besides "In addition to, as well as." **He has plenty to do besides study**.

be sure and **Be sure to** is the correct form.

between Say **between you and me**, never *between you and I*. See also AMONG.

bi-weekly This tricky word can mean "twice a week" or even "every two weeks," so we never know what to believe when we see or hear it. In your own speech, it's better to use **bi-weekly** for "every two weeks" and **semi-weekly** for "twice a week."

boat "A small vessel." An oceanliner, or any other big vessel, is not a *boat* but a **ship**.

both alike Say simply **they are alike**. You don't need the *both*.

boy Do not use to refer to a man.

bring In the sense of conveying, **bring** indicates movement toward the speaker. Example: **Bring the book to me**. The sentence *Bring this form when you go to the doctor's office* is wrong. It should be **take**.

bust Avoid saying *bust* when you mean **burst**.

but This word is not needed after *doubt* and *help*. Say **I don't doubt that** rather than *I don't doubt but that*.

check into, check out	Usually **check** is sufficient. You do, of course, **check into** your hotel and go to the **check out** counter.
claim	This word is not to be used as a substitute for **say**. Wrong: *She claimed I did it.* Right: **She said I did it.**
class	Do not use this word to describe style (it shows a lack of it). *She really has class* shows that the speaker has none.
clean, clear	These words should not be used to describe degree. *Clean up to here* and *clear up to here* should be eliminated.
come	Do not use this word instead of **came**. The past tense of *come* is came. **I came to the party early.**
come and	Say **come to**: **Come to see me tomorrow.**
compare with, compare to	**Compare with** is used with two things or people of equal stature, perhaps to point out differences. **Compare to** means "liken to" and is used for fanciful comparisons: **"Shall I compare thee to a summer's day?"** Or: **He compared his teacher to Socrates.**
comptroller	A variant of the word **controller**. Used as the title for a financial officer. Pronounce the same as **controller**.
convince	**Convince** is used with **of** or **that**. Avoid using with *to*. One may persuade someone to do something—in fact, **persuade** can be used with all three constructions.
couple	We need to exercise care in the pluralization of this word. Say two couples, not *two couple.*
crass	The original and still preferred meaning here is "stupid." The word sounds like **brassy, gross,** and **crude**, but these are very new meanings.
criterion, criteria	A **criterion** is a standard test by which

something is compared or measured. The plural is **criteria**, often used incorrectly as the singular.

datum, data The word **datum**, rarely used, means a "fact." The plural form is **data**. Although **data** is widely used for both the singular and plural, it is comforting to know the difference.

decimate This is from the Latin *decem,* "ten." It means, literally, to "select by lot and kill one in every ten." Many people use it incorrectly to mean "the killing of a large number," or "total destruction."

did, done Avoid *I have did.* Say simply, **I did**. The word **have** must be followed by **done**, as in **I have done my work**. Likewise, never say *I done.*

differ **Differ with** a person; **differ from** something; **differ on** an issue.

different **Different from** is the correct form. *Different than* is to be avoided, although **other than** is all right.

discover Do not use interchangeably with **invent**. **Discover** means "to learn of"; **invent** means "to originate."

distrust "Lack of trust." It has the same meaning as **mistrust**.

done Not interchangeable with **finish**. If you say **The painting will be done next week**, it is unclear whether you mean "someone will be painting next week," or "by next week the painting will be completed."

disinterested "Impartial, objective." A judge should be a **disinterested** listener. (He should not take sides.) If you mean "having no interest in," say **uninterested. He was an uninterested student; he did a lot of daydreaming.**

draught Chiefly British. Pronunciation and meaning identical to **draft**.

drug This is not the past tense of **drag**. Say **dragged**. **She dragged the child out of the room.**

each A singular word. When used in a sentence it must be matched with other singular words. Say **each brought his own** (not *their own*). Since **their** is plural, it is correctly used as follows: **They brought their own.** The plural **their** matches the plural **they**.

eager "Desirous of something." Do not confuse with *anxious*.

end product Just say **product** (unless you need to distinguish something from an intermediate product).

enough Guard against inserting *enough* when it is not needed. *We were fortunate enough to receive the gift* is strengthened by saying simply, **We were fortunate to receive the gift**.

et Not to be used when you mean **eaten**. Say **we have eaten**, never *we et*.

et cetera Never say *and et cetera*. *Et* is Latin for **and**.

everybody . . . their **Everybody** is still singular and takes a singular pronoun: **Everybody had his or her own umbrella at last.** If that elaborate **his or her** bothers you, say **We all had our own** or **They all had their own.**

everyplace Not when you mean **everywhere**. In sentences such as **Every place was taken**, it is two words.

except You'll do all right if you remember to use **me, him**, and **her** after **except**, in sentences such as **No one loved you except me**, and, similarly, **No one loves him except her.**

feel — When used as a substitute for **think** or **believe**, make sure it fits the context better, and you are not using it just to hedge.

female — When referring to human beings, do not use this word as a noun. You may refer to a **group of women**, but not to a *group of females*. It is all right to refer to animals as **females**.

fewer — An adjective meaning "a smaller number." Say **There are fewer children in school**, not *there are less children*. See LESS.

fit — The past tense of this verb is **fitted**.

flammable, inflammable — **Flammable** and **inflammable** are the same in usage and meaning. See NONFLAMMABLE. (One oil company avoids the problems by putting "COMBUSTIBLE" on the sides of its trucks.)

foot/feet — It is all right to say **a six-foot rug**. But a man is **six feet tall**, not *six foot*.

former — Use **former** to refer to the first of two things. Use **first** to refer to the first of more than two things. **Nicky Hilton was Elizabeth Taylor's first husband.**

froze — Do not say *I am froze*. Say either **I froze** or **I am frozen**.

gal — Many women are campaigning against the use of the word *gal*. **Woman** is preferred.

gift — By definition, a gift is free. Do not say *a free gift*.

girl — Do not use the word **girl** to refer to a woman.

give — The past tense of this word is **gave. I gave it to him yesterday**. Never, never say *I have gave*. When paired with **have**, the correct form is **given. I have given it to him**.

good/well — Instead of getting into the *I feel good/I*

feel well dilemma, say **I am well**. It's easier.

got   Do not use when you mean **have**. Wrong: *I got my book with me*. Right: **I have my book with me**.

graduate   You can **graduate from a school**, or **be graduated from a school**. You cannot *graduate it,* however, unless you have been given the responsibility of dividing it into grades. *He graduated high school* shows that the speaker probably did not.

grammatical   "According to the rules of grammar." Accordingly, we don't say *grammatical errors* but, rather, **errors in grammar**.

hanged   A man is **hanged**. A picture is **hung**.

hardly   Guard against using with other negative words; **hardly** is already negative. And two negatives cancel each other. Say **can hardly**, not *can't hardly*.

home   Not to be used interchangeably with **house**. The latter refers to a dwelling. Sometimes a **home** can be created there.

human   Pronounced **hyoo'•mun**, this is an adjective, often describing the word **being**, as in **human being**. *Human* as a noun is common only in science fiction. (Sound the **h**.)

hung   A picture is **hung**. A man is **hanged**.

I   Use **I** only as the subject of a sentence (**I like this**) or after **is** and **was** (**It is I**).

I been   The correct way to say this is **I have been**.

index   The preferred plural form of this word is **indexes**, except in mathematics, where **indices** is common.

individual   Should not be used indiscriminately for "person." **Person** may be applied to anyone as a general term. An individual is a particular being.

infamous   Pronounced **in'•fa•mus**, this word means

	"disgraceful, having a bad reputation." It does not mean *unknown*.
innovation	Do not put *new* in front of this word: If something is innovative, it is new.
invaluable	"Too valuable to be measured." Do not use when you mean **valuable**.
invent	"To originate something." Compare with DISCOVER.
invite	A verb. Do not use as a noun; that is, you receive an **invitation**, not an *invite*.
join together	Just say **join**. You don't need to add *together*. (The use of **join together** *is* acceptable in marriage ceremonies.)
kind	Say **that kind** or **those kinds**. Do not say *those kind*.
knot	This word has several meanings, one of which is "a unit of speed." The words *an hour* should never follow it. A ship can travel at six knots or at six nautical miles per hour, but *not* at *six knots per hour*.
kudos	Pronounced **koo' dahs** or **koo' dos**. This Greek word means "glory or fame." The final **s** is not the sign of a plural: no such thing exists as *a kudo*. **Kudos** is singular: **Kudos was due the first astronaut.**
lay/lie	In the present tense, the verb **lay** needs an object: **Hens lay eggs. Lay the book on the table.** Lay is also the *past* tense of the verb **lie**, meaning "to assume a reclining position." **I want to lie down. Please lie down. Let's lie out in the sun. I lay down yesterday.** (If the verb **lie** refers to the telling of a falsehood, the past tense is **lied**, as in **He lied to me.**)
learn	Do not use *learn* when you mean **teach**. A student learns. A teacher teaches. You cannot *learn* someone how to do something, but you can **teach** him.

leave   This word usually means "to depart." **Leave without me.** Do not confuse it with the word **let,** which usually means "to permit." Correct: **Let it stand the way it is. Let go of me.** But not *Leave go of me.*

legalistic   Not interchangeable with **legal. Legalistic** implies a stricter application to the law than does **legal.**

lend   As a verb this word is preferred over **loan.** The latter has been established as a verb in business usage; however, it is still preferable to keep the forms separate. **She asked her father for a loan, and he lent her the amount she needed.**

less   An adjective or an adverb meaning "not so much." **There is less milk left than I thought.** Say **fewer** when you refer to something that can be counted. See FEWER.

liable   Pronounced **li'•u•bl**, this word means "legally responsible, or probable (in the sense of something impending, usually dangerous or unpleasant)." **Reckless motorists are liable to suffer injuries.** Do not use as a substitute for *likely.*

like   "Equally, in the same manner." Use **like** before nouns or pronouns. Do not substitute *as,* which is used before a phrase or clause. See AS.

likely   "Probable." **The moon is likely to come out tonight.** The word has no negative connotation, as does *liable.*

lines of communication   Usually preferred over *line of communications.*

lit   The latest dictionaries sanction this usage as a past tense form of **to light,** although **lighted** remains the more accepted form. **Lit** is all right when used as an adjective: **The candles are lit.**

livid   "Bluish," as a **livid** bruise.

loan   See LEND.

lots of   **Many** is preferred.

mad   **Mad** means "crazy or frenzied." Do not use when you mean **angry**.

male   Do not use as a noun. **Male** is acceptable as a noun only with reference to animals.

maltreat, mistreat   These two words are interchangeable.

me   Use it with confidence. Do not substitute **I** as the object of a verb or preposition. Say **between you and me. They came to see Bruce and me.** Do not use **me** as a subject. It is incorrect to say *Me and John are going* or *John and me are going.*

media   This is the plural of **medium**. Say **Radio and television are popular media. But Radio remains a popular medium.** When **medium** refers to someone with psychic abilities, the plural is **mediums.**

mile   It is all right to say **one mile,** but with two or more miles it is necessary to add that **s.** One may refer to a **ten-mile drive.** But do not say *I live ten mile from here.*

most   Do not substitute for **almost.** The misuse of *most* for **very** occurs more often in written than in spoken English, but beware of sentences like *He was most cooperative,* when "he" is not being compared with anyone.

my   Possessive case of the pronoun **I.** Say **This is my book.** Also say **He objected to my going.** Do not say *Do you mind me going without you?"*

myself   You can use this word to refer *back* to yourself (**I dressed myself**) or for emphasis (**I'd rather do it myself.**) When it is incorrectly used, it hurts many ears. Wrong: *He asked Bruce and myself.* Say **He asked**

Bruce and me. Wrong: *Bruce and myself are undecided.*

never Means "not ever." Do not use when you mean **not**. *Who spilled the milk? I never did it!* implies that you have never in your life spilled milk.

none Means "no one." Say **None of us is ready**. **None** is a singular subject. It demands a singular verb to match.

nonflammable Since **flammable** and **inflammable** are interchangeable, use **nonflammable** to mean "will not burn."

number Use **number** to refer to items that can be counted; use **amount** to refer to a general quantity. **A number of people were present. I need a large amount of sugar.** See AMOUNT.

of Not a substitute for **have**. Do not say *I would of gone,* or *I wish I could of been there,* or *you shouldn't of said that*. It is **would have, could have, should have.**

oral Oral means "spoken." It is not interchangeable with **verbal**. **Verbal** can mean "spoken" or it can refer to something that is written.

other than Not *different than,* although you may say **different from**.

out With **hide, win,** and **lose,** *out* is superfluous.

over Instead of saying *Over forty members were there,* say **More than forty members were there.**

over with Omit the *with.*

pair, pairs The plural of **pair** is **pairs. I plan to take two pairs of shoes.** Never say *two pair.*

party Usually refers to more than one person. Exceptions: telephone and legal usage.

peer In Britain a **peer** is a nobleman. But in

this country a **peer** is one who has equal standing with another. Do not use when you refer to a superior.

phase Means "state of transition or development." It is not to be used to mean *aspect* or *topic*.

phenomena This is the plural of **phenomenon**, "a visible occurrence or one that is extraordinary or marvelous." Do not use **phenomena** when speaking of only one such occurrence.

pimento, pimiento Both spellings are acceptable, and both are pronounced **pi•men'•to**.

preventative **Preventive** is preferred. Many Cincinnati doctors swear there was once a University of Cincinnati professor of preventive medicine who would flunk a student who said *preventative*.

proved As the past tense of **prove**, preferred over *proven*. **It has been proved.** It is acceptable to use **proven** as an adjective: **a proven fact**.

provided Preferred over *providing* when used to mean "on the condition that." **We will go provided it doesn't rain.**

quarter of, quarter to When referring to time, it is correct to say **a quarter to three**. In the case of money one says **a quarter of a dollar**.

quash "To put down or suppress completely." Not to be used in a milder sense. **The revolution was quashed.**

quick An adjective meaning "speedy." It is not acceptable to most experts when used as an adverb. They cringe if they see or hear *Come quick*. Add the **-ly** to make it right.

refined This word should not be used to describe people. Sugar is **refined**.

regard "To consider." **Regard** also means "to

hold in high esteem." It can be used to mean "reference," as in **with regard to your question**. *With regards to* is incorrect.

regards "Greetings." This word is not considered to be interchangeable with **respect** (in the sense of **with respect to**). Nor is it interchangeable with **regard**.

relator A **relator** narrates an account or story. Do not use when you mean **Realtor**, a real estate agent affiliated with the National Association of Real Estate Boards. (Not all real estate agents are Realtors.)

rob *He robbed my pencil* is bad English. A person can be **robbed**, but his possessions are **stolen**.

run The past tense is **ran. I ran yesterday**, not *I run yesterday*. However, it is correct to say **I have run**.

sanatarium "A health resort." The word **sanatorium**, which used to refer to a mental institution, now can have the same meaning as **sanatarium**; however, it should be noted that there is still an aura of the old meaning hovering around **sanatorium**.

saw One should not put **have** in front of this word. Say **I saw**, not *I have saw*. Also correct: **I have seen**. See SEEN.

scarcely Avoid using with another negative word, as **scarcely** is already negative, and two negatives cancel each other out. Say **can scarcely**, not *can't* scarcely. Say **I can scarcely**, rather than *I can't scarcely*.

scissors Plural in form and used with a plural verb. We usually refer to **a pair of scissors**. But **Where are the scissors?**

seen Avoid saying *I seen*. It is **I have seen** or **I saw**. See SAW.

should of Incorrect way of saying **should have**.

simultaneous Do not use to describe an action, but only to describe a thing or things. It is a **simultaneous occurrence** if two things happen simultaneously.

sinus Something everybody has—so do not announce that you *have sinus*. You probably mean that you are having **sinus inflammation** or **sinus discomfort**.

snuck No. The past tense of **sneak** is **sneaked**. **He sneaked around the house.**

strata The plural form of **stratum**. It means "layers." You may refer to **every stratum of society**, but you would say **all strata of society**.

suite Pronounced **sweet**. It means "a succession of related things: a series of connected rooms; a matched set of furniture." Please note: You may have a *suit* of clothes, but you own a **suite** of furniture.

suspicion If you suspect something, you have a **suspicion**. Do not say *I suspicion*.

swum The past tense of **I swim** is **I swam**, or you may say **I have swum**. You may also use **swum** when speaking of distance **to be swum**.

take Use **take** to indicate movement away from the speaker. Example: **Take the book to him.** Compare with BRING.

temperature Tem'•pur•ah•chur. The degree of hotness or coldness. Since everybody has one, it sounds a bit naïve to announce brightly, *I have a temperature*. If you want to tell us about it, report on whether it is above or below normal. Or simply say **I have a fever**.

tract Do not say *tract* when you mean track.

transpire Careful writers do not use **transpire** when they mean *happen* or *come to pass*. Trans-

pire means "to be revealed, to become known," as in **We had to wait until after the war for the secret to transpire.**

trivia Plural. It is wrong to say, *I don't enjoy talking about this trivia,* and *these trivia* sounds stilted. **These trivial matters** is all right. But if it's the what's-the-name-of-Buck-Rogers'-horse variety you're talking about, you're better off keeping away from all words that require a singular or plural form. No one ever says *a trivium,* either.

try and Say **try to** rather than *try and;* for example, **Try to come along.** See AND.

undersigned This word seems stuffy to most people, but it is perfectly acceptable, so use it where indicated—usually only in written legal documents or other official letters or agreements.

unique Means "the only one of its kind." It is incorrect to say *most unique* or *very unique.*

up This is standard English, but it frequently *turns up* when not needed. Words such as **add, head, start, think,** and **wait** are stronger when you don't put *up* after them. It doesn't belong before **until** either.

utilize **To utilize something** is to "find use for something already in service or to expand productivity by finding new uses." Do not substitute **utilize** for **use** if it does not have one of these meanings.

valuable "Having value." Compare with INVALUABLE.

via The meaning is usually restricted to "by way of," rather than *"by means of."*

virus You can't *have a virus* the way you **have a**

                cold. A virus is smaller than a germ, and when you're ill with a virus attack, you may have more than one virus.

wait on   Do not use when you mean **wait for**. A valet may **wait on** his master, but you do not *wait on* a friend unless you are serving him. Say **I am waiting for him**.

way   Take care to say **a way** when your meaning is singular: **Phyllis has a long way to go.** Add the **s** only when you refer to more than one way: **There are two ways to look at it.**

went   *Have* should never appear in front of **went. I went**, or **I have gone.**

wore out   It is all right to say **I wore out my shoes.** It is not acceptable to say *I'm wore out*. Say **I'm worn out**, or, better still, **I'm tired.**

would   Almost everyone deplores the use of *would of* for **would have**, and of *if he would have* for **if he had**.

wrench   "A tool." Or, if used as a verb, it means to "twist violently." It does not mean to "rinse."

Xmas   Although **X** represents the Greek letter **chi**, a symbol for Christ, this abbreviation is offensive to some Christians.

yet   Use only when it increases the clarity of a sentence; avoid the unnecessary *yet*. It is better to say **Have you washed?** than *Have you washed yet?*

yourself   **Yourself** is not interchangeable with **you**. It is right to say **I plan to invite Gloria and you**, and wrong to say *I plan to invite Gloria and yourself*. See MYSELF.

UNMATCHED PAIRS

Many of these word couples have nothing in common but their sound, whereas some are similar in meaning but not identical. Learn to distinguish them and you will have found another way of improving your spoken English.

abjure/adjure   To **abjure** something is to "repudiate or renounce" it. **Adjure** means "command or entreat."

adverse/averse   **Adverse** means "detrimental in design or effect": **The medication caused an adverse reaction. Averse** means "strongly disinclined."

advice/advise   One offers **advice** (noun) when one **advises** (verb).

affect/effect   **Affect** means to "influence." The result is an **effect. Effect** is also a verb meaning "to bring about; cause." (By the way, there is a noun **affect** in psychology, meaning a "feeling or emotion." It is pronounced with the accent on the first syllable.)

allude/elude   **Allude** means "refer obliquely." **Elude** means to "evade."

allusion/illusion   An **allusion** is an indirect reference. Don't confuse with **illusion**: "an unreal image, a false impression." And never use **allusion** for a direct reference; just say **reference**.

alternately/alternative   To **alternate** is to "go back and forth between two things"; thus, **alternately** means "as an occasional substitute." An **alternative** is an "option," and is the proper word to introduce a second, or even third, possibility. See ALTERNATIVE, in Usage section.

assure/ensure   To **assure** is "to state with confidence that something has been or will be accomplished." **Ensure** is to "make certain of something." (**Insure** is reserved for the insurance-company kind of **insure**.)

avenge/revenge   To **avenge** means to "exact justice." It is often confused with the word **revenge**, which means to "retaliate." If you will remember that **revenge** and **retaliate** both start with **re-**, you won't have any more trouble with these words. The corresponding nouns are **vengeance** and **revenge**.

beside/besides   **Beside** means "at the side of, alongside." Do not use *of* after the word **beside**. **Besides** means "in addition to, as well as."

biannual/biennial   The first means "twice a year" and is interchangeable with **semiannual**. The second means "every two years."

Calvary/cavalry   **Calvary** is the place near Jerusalem where Christ was crucified. **Cavalry** has to do with horses. I always remember the distinction between these two by associating **Calvin**, the Christian reformer, with the first and the word **cavalier** with the second.

cement/concrete   The first is dry; the second is first wet and then dry. **Concrete** is a mixture of **cement**, sand, gravel, and water.

censor/censure   A **censor** is "one who examines or judges." As a verb, **censor** means to "examine or assess." A **censure** is an "expression of disapproval." As a verb, it means "to express disapproval."

childish/childlike   **Childish** means "of, similar to, or suitable for a child." When used to describe an adult, the word often connotes foolishness. **Childlike** is a more positive word, meaning "like, or befitting, a child; innocent."

climactic/climatic   **Climactic** means "pertaining to a climax." **Climatic** has to do with conditions of climate.

collaborate/ corroborate   Remember that the word **labor** is contained in **collaborate** and you'll remember that it means "work together." To **corroborate** is to "confirm or strengthen." **He corroborated her testimony.**

comprise/constitute	**Comprise** means "embrace"—there's a vivid image for you. Remember it and you'll never say *the seven people who comprise the committee.* They **constitute** it. Or, **The committee comprises seven members.**
connive/contrive	**Connive** originally meant (and in precise usage still means) to "shut one's eyes to a crime." Possibly by confusion with **contrive**, it has come to be misused for the perpetration of the crime itself. The right word to use for a criminal act involving plotting is **conspire**.
contemptible/ contemptuous	**Contemptible** means "deserving of contempt"; **contemptuous** means "having contempt for."
continual/continuous	**Continual** means "again and again"; **continuous**, "without interruption."
credible/credulous	**Credible** means "believable." **Credulous** means "gullible, ready to believe." (**Creditable** has nothing to do with believing; it means "deserving of credit or praise.")
deprecate/depreciate	**Deprecate** is often misused for **depreciate**. **Deprecate** means "to seek to avert by supplication," or "to disapprove." To **depreciate** is to "lower in value." The phrase *self-deprecating remarks* is best altered to **self-belittling** or **self-disparaging** remarks.
distrait/distraught	**Distrait**, pronounced **dis•trā'**, means "absent-minded, inattentive." **Distraught** means "distracted, harassed."
elicit/illicit	To **elicit** is to "draw forth, to evoke." **Illicit** is an adjective meaning "illegal or unlawful."
emigrate/immigrate	Remember that **immigrate** and **in** both start with an **i**, and you may remember that **immigrate** means "to go into a country"; **emigrate**, "to leave it."
eminent/imminent	**Eminent** means "high in station or esteem"; **imminent** means "about to happen."

farther/further	**Farther** refers to measurable distance. **Their house is farther away than we thought. Further,** as an adjective, describes "a continuation, usually of time or degree." **She had further news.** (As a verb it means "to advance," as in **to further a career.**)
fiscal/physical	**Fiscal,** pronounced **fis'•kul,** means "of or pertaining to finance." **Physical, fiz'•u•kul,** means "pertaining to the body."
flaunt/flout	To **flaunt** is to "show off"; to **flout** is to "scorn, to scoff at, to show contempt for."
formally/formerly	**Formally** means "in a strict or formal manner"; **formerly** means "previously."
healthful/healthy	**Healthful** means "health-giving"; **healthy** means "possessing health." It is therefore erroneous to speak of a *healthy walk in the mountains* or *glass of milk*—these things are **healthful.**
historic/historical	**Historic** means "important or famous in history; having influence on history." **The walk on the moon was a historic event.** In contrast, **historical** means "based on history." You may speak of a **historical novel** or a **historical fact,** but not a *historical occurrence.*
imply/infer	Speakers and writers **imply** something by what they say; they do not *infer.* The listeners or readers **infer** something from the remarks of the speakers or writers. Do not say *are you inferring* when you mean **are you implying.**
impracticable/ impractical	**Impracticable** means "not capable of being carried out; unreasonably difficult of performance." Something that is **impractical** is "not a wise thing to implement or do."
ingenious/ingenuous	**Ingenious,** pronounced **in•jee'•nyus,** means "resourceful, clever, inventive,

adroit." The slightly rarer **ingenuous, in•jen'•yoo•us,** means "frank, open, honest."

languishing/lavishing The first means "fading away, growing weak," as in **He was languishing in the tropical climate.** Lavishing means "laying generously upon," often used with **praise: to lavish with praise.**

limp/limpid Everyone knows what **limp** means. Beware of saying **limpid** for anything but "clear": **Her eyes were limpid jewels of blue.**

loose/lose Loose, pronounced **loos,** means "not confined or restrained; free." To **lose,** pronounced **looz,** is to "mislay," or "not to win."

luxuriant/luxurious The first means "overgrown, as a forest; full." The second, much more common, means "rich; elegant; commodious."

marital/martial Marital, pronounced **mair'•i•tul,** means "pertaining to marriage." **Martial** means "of war; suitable for war; warlike," and is pronounced **mahr'•shul.**

meantime/meanwhile Remember "meanwhile, back at the ranch," and you won't confuse these two. **Meanwhile** is an adverb, a word used to describe an action; **meantime** is a noun. Therefore, you can't say *in the meanwhile* or *meantime, back at the ranch.*

moral/morale Moral, "ethical, virtuous," is pronounced **maw'•rul. Morale, maw•ral',** means "the state of the spirits of an individual or group."

nauseated/nauseous Nauseated means "feeling nausea"; **nauseous** means "causing nausea." **It was a nauseous situation.** Do not say *I feel nauseous;* rather, say **I am nauseated.**

noisome/noisy Noisome means "offensive, particularly with reference to odors." Do not use it to mean "somewhat noisy."

partial/partly	**Partial** refers to preference. It is not interchangeable with **partly**.
persecute/prosecute	Both words describe negative actions by one person toward another, but **persecute** means "to oppress, annoy, molest, bother." **Prosecute** means to "sue, indict, arraign, follow, pursue."
prostate/prostrate	The first is a gland. **Prostrate** means "stretched out, prone; powerless, resigned." By the way, don't confuse **prone** ("lying face down") with **supine** ("lying face up").
purposefully/ purposely	The first means "with purpose and determination"; the second, "intentionally."
ravage/ravish	Both have something to do with violence, but **ravage** means "destroy" and **ravish** means "rape or violate."
regime/regimen	**Regime** means "rule"; **regimen** means "routine." So you don't follow a *regime of diet and exercise;* it's a **regimen**.
regretfully/regrettably	**Regretfully** describes the feeling of regret; **regrettably** expresses the fact that something is worthy of regret.
rend/render	To **rend** is to "tear." **Render** means to "give, deliver, impart; melt."
sensual/sexual	**Sensual** refers to the senses—taste, feel, smell, sight, hearing—and their gratification. **Sexual** refers to sex and reproduction.
tack/tact	A **tack** is a short light nail with a sharp point. **Tact** is the ability to do or say the most diplomatic or fitting thing. They should *not* be pronounced the same way.
tortuous/torturous	**Tortuous**: "winding, twisting, circuitous," as in **It was a tortuous road. Torturous**, less frequently used, means "painful."
turbid/turgid	**Turbid** means "clouded; muddied." **Turgid** means "inflated, stiff."

venal/venial	**Venal** means "susceptible to bribery; corruptible." Do not confuse with **venial**, which, although it sometimes has to do with describing sin, means "excusable, pardonable."
wangle/wrangle	**Wangle** means "to get by contrivance; to manipulate." Do not confuse with **wrangle**, which means "to bicker; to herd horses or other livestock."

3

PRONUNCIATION PITFALLS

Pronunciation is a difficult area of speech for most of us because we don't really listen to ourselves. "Proof *heed*ing" our speech is every bit as tricky as proofreading something we've written.

Participants in my Word Watchers' Clinic assure me they have mastered pitfalls in pronunciation by following the suggestions below. You can too.

1. *Use the "buddy system." Ask your spouse (who probably has your errors on tap), a fellow student, a coworker, your child, or a friend to help you spot your mistakes. Do the same for her or him if asked.*
2. *Read each pronunciation given here as though you had never seen the word before. Remember this is a special list. It consists of mispronunciations considered errors by the hundreds of contributors to this book.*
3. *If you have access to a tape recorder, by all means use it. Hear yourself as others do. Record the correct pronunciations of words that trouble you. Practice the pronunciation until you have mastered it. You can also record talk shows or educational material and play them back to make sure you have understood every word.*
4. *Check in an unabridged dictionary the pronunciation of each new word you hear.*
5. *Make flash cards of words you frequently mispronounce.*

Keep the cards with you until you can pronounce each word as automatically as you say "dog" and "cat."

This chapter is a list of words that are frequently mispronounced. Learn the ones that you have trouble with—and be honest. Then make it a lifetime habit to let no word go unturned; that is, turn those dictionary pages. Learn each new word and *practice* it until you're able to use it naturally. The rewards to your self-confidence will make it worthwhile.

Pronunciation Key

a	as in **dad**	ī	as in **bite**
ā	as in **day**	ō	as in **oat**
ah	as in **father**	oo	as in **fool**
ai	as in **care**	o͞o	as in **look**
au	as in **now**	oi	as in **boy**
aw	as in **cross**	ur	as in **her**
e	as in **set**	u	as in **luck**
ee	as in **beet**	g	as in **girl**
g	as in **age**	j	as in **jam**
i	as in **bit**	zh	as in **vision**

absorb	**ab•sawrb'** is preferred over *ab•zawb'*.
absurd	"Contrary to common sense; ludicrous." It's pronounced **ab•surd'**, not *ab•zurd'*.
accessory	"Anything that contributes in a secondary way," as **accessories** to a costume. The first **c** is pronounced as a **k: ak•ses'•saw•ree**.
across	**ah•craws'** There is no **t** sound in this word.
acumen	**a•kyoo'•men**.
adult	Stress the second syllable, not the first: **a•dult'**.
aged	When you use it as an adjective, pronounce both syllables: **an ā'•jed person**.

	When you use it as a verb, pronounce it as one syllable: **a person who ājd rapidly.**
á la mode	"To the manner, to the way." Not limited to the ice cream on top of your pie. Say **ah•lah•mōd′.**
almond	**ah′•muhnd.**
alumna	Originally Latin (feminine form of **alumnus**). "A girl or woman who has attended or been graduated from a school or college." The plural form is **alumnae** (pronounced **ah•lum•nee′**).
alumnus	From the Latin. "A boy or man who has attended or been graduated from a school or college." **Alumni (ah•lum•nī′)** is the plural form.
amateur	**am′•u•tur.** Not **am′•u•chur.**
ambassador	**am•bas′•u•dur.** Not *am•bas′•u•dawr.*
anti-	As in **antibiotic** and other words, it sounds better to say **an′•tee** than **an′•tī.**
apartheid	**uh•part•hāt.** Say it as though it ended with a **t** instead of **d.** It refers to an official policy of racial segregation.
apricot	**ap′•ri•caht.**
arctic	**ahrk′•tic.** Pronounce that **c** in the middle.
aspirin	**as′•pur•in.** There are three syllables to the word. Avoid the *aspern* and *asprin* pronunciations.
athletics	**ath•le′•tiks.** This word has three syllables, never four.
auxiliary	Pronounce **aug•zil′•ya•ree.** Make that four syllables.
baklava	That Middle Eastern honey-and-nut pastry is **bah•klah•vah′.**
barbiturate	Sound the second **r.**
basis	Means "foundation." Remember that the plural form is **bases**, pronounced **bay′•seez.**

Beaujolais	Say **bō•zhō•lä'**. This is a red table wine.
berserk	**bur•surk'**. Sound both **r**'s.
bisect	**bī•sect'**.
boatswain	Pronounced **bo'•sun**. "A petty officer in charge of a ship."
borrow	Rhymes with **sorrow**. Avoid the *borry* pronunciation of the word.
bouillon	**boo'•yun**. "A clear broth or soup." Note BULLION.
bovine	Make the second syllable rhyme with **wine: bo'•vīn**. It means "like a cow."
brouhaha	**broo•hah'•hah**. "Hubbub, uproar."
bruit	**To bruit something about** is "to tell it; to let the word travel about." Pronounced **broot**—one syllable.
brut	"Dry, as champagne." Also **broot**—pronounce the **t**.
bullion	**bul'•yun**. "Gold or silver uncoined or in a mass."
cabinet	**kab'•in•et**. Three syllables.
calliope	**ka•lī'•ō•pee**. "A musical instrument whose pipes are sounded by steam pressure, used on riverboats and in circuses."
canapé	**kan'•u•pā**. "An appetizer."
caramel	**kair'•u•mel**.
Caucasian	**kaw•kā'•zhen**.
chafe	**chāf**. "To make sore by rubbing."
chaff	**chaf**. "The external envelopes, or husks, of grain."
chasm	**kaz'•um**. Sound that "**k**." A chasm is a yawning hollow, a deep gorge.
chassis	**shas'•ee**.
chic	**sheek**, not *chick* or *shick*.
chimney	**chim'•nee**. It has two syllables, not three, and an **n**, not an **i**, after the **m**.
chiropodist	**ki•rah'•pe•dist**. "One who treats foot ail-

ments." Remember to pronounce the word as though it started with a **k**.

chocolate All right to pronounce it as you did when a child—**chawk'•lit**.

coiffure Pronounce it **kwah•fyoor'**.

colonel **kur'•nul**.

comely **kum'•lee**. "Of pleasing appearance." Does not rhyme with **homely**.

comptroller A variant of the word **controller**. Used as the title for a financial officer. Pronounce it **kun•tro'•lur**.

conch **kahnk** or **kanch**.

congratulate **cun•gra'•tyoo•lāt**. Be sure to sound the **t** in the middle of the word.

connoisseur **kahn•u•sur'**. "A competent judge of art or in matters of taste."

consummate When you use the word as a verb, pronounce it **kahn'•su•māt**. When you use it as an adjective, meaning "extremely skilled," say **kahn'•soo•mit**.

creek **kreek**. "A small stream of water, a brook," Do not confuse with **crick**.

crick **krik** (rhymes with **sick**). "A muscle spasm."

cuisine **kwi•zeen'**. "Style or quality of cooking."

culinary **kyoo'•li•nair•ee**. "Of or pertaining to cooking or the kitchen."

dais If you spell it correctly, you'll probably pronounce it correctly. It is **dā'•is**. The **a** has a long sound.

data, datum **dāt'•ah; dāt'•um**. Data is the plural form of **datum**. Although **data** is widely used for both, it is comforting to know the difference.

deaf **def**. Avoid the *deef* pronunciation.

debacle **dā•bah'•kul**. "Sudden collapse; rout."

December	The word is not *Dezember*. Please do not sound a **z** in the pronunciation.
decrepit	It's a **t** on the end, not a **d**.
dentifrice	**den′•tu•fris.** Do not say *den′•tur•fris.*
despicable	**des•pik′•u•bul.** Means "contemptible."
desultory	**de′•zul•taw•ree.** "Random; now and then."
détente	"An agreement between nations to relax or ease aggression; its purpose is to reduce tension." Pronounce it **dā•tahnt′**.
detritus	**de•trī′•tus.** dĕ trī′ tus. Loose particles or fragments.
diamond	**dī′•u•mund.** Let's hear all three syllables.
diaper	**dī•u•pur.** It has three syllables.
dilettante	**dil•uh•tant′.** "One who dabbles in many things but masters none."
diphtheria	**dif•thir′•ee•u.** No *dip* sound in this word.
dirigible	**dur′•u•ju•bl.**
draught	Chiefly British. Pronunciation and meaning interchangeable with **draft**.
dreamed, dreamt	**dreemed; dremt.** Either of these words is correct.
ecstasy	**ek′•stah•see.**
ecumenism	**ek′•yoo•mēn′iz′um.**
elm	This word has one syllable; do not make it *el′•lum.*
ennui	**ahn•wee′.** Means "boredom, listlessness."
en route	**ahn•root′.** "On or along the way."
entree	**ahn′•trā′.** "The right to enter," or "the main course of a meal."
envelope	**en′•vah•lōp** if a noun; **en•vel′•up** if a verb.
environment	**en•vī•run•ment.** Let's hear that **n** in the middle.
epicurean	**ep•i•kyoor•ee′•an.**
err	**ur.**

escape	**es•cāp'**. There is no **x** in this word.
espresso	**es•pres'•sō**. Not *ex•pres'•sō*.
et cetera	**et•set'•ur•u**. Never say *ek•set'•ur•u*.
experiment	**ek•sper'•u•ment**. There is no *spear* in this word.
faux pas	"A blunder." Say **fō•pah'**, or else you will demonstrate what it is.
February	**Feb'•roo•a•ree**. Please pronounce both **r**'s.
fiancé	**fee•ahn'•sā**. Pronounce this as you would the feminine word **fiancée**.
field	Be sure to sound the **d** at the end of the word.
fifth	There is an **f** in the middle.
film	The word has one syllable; do not say *fil'•um*. Or *flim*.
fiscal	**fis'•kul**. "Of or pertaining to finance." Do not confuse with physical.
fission	**fizh'•un**. Not **fish'•in**.
flaccid	**flak'•sid**. "Flabby."
flautist, flutist	**flau'•tist** is preferred. The first syllable rhymes with **now**.
forbade	The past tense of **forbid** is pronounced **for•bad'**.
forte	"That which one does most easily." It has one syllable (say **fawrt**); unless, of course, you're using the musical **forte** (meaning "loud"), and then you say **fawr'tā**.
foyer	**fwah•yā'** was the original pronunciation, although most dictionaries accept **foy'•ur**.
fracas	**fra'•kus**. "A noisy quarrel."
gauche	**gōsh**. "Clumsy, tactless."
genealogy	**jee•nee•ahl'•u•jee**. Please note the **a** in the middle of the word.
genuine	**jen'•yoo•in**. Avoid making the last syllable rhyme with **vine**.
giant	Pronounced **jī'•ant**, not *jīnt*.
giblet	**jib•lut**.

government	**gu'•vurn•ment.** Be sure to sound the **n** in the middle.
granted	**gran•ted.** One should be able to take for granted that this word will not be confused with **granite**.
grievous	**gree'•vus.**
grocery	**grō'•sir•ee.** Make it three syllables.
guarantee	**gair•un•tee'.** The first syllable rhymes with **air**.
gynecology	You pronounce the **g** as you do in **girl**. It is **gī•nu•kahl'•u•jee**.
hallucinogen	**ha•loo'•si•ne•jen.** Confusing, because in **carcinogen** the accent is on the **sin**.
harass	**har'•us.** "To disturb or irritate." The accent is preferred on the first syllable.
harbinger	**hahr'•bin•jur.** Something that is a sign of what is to come.
height	**hīte.** Rhymes with **kite**.
help	Let's hear that l. The word is **help**, not *hep*.
herb	The preferred pronunciation is **urb**. Note that you do sound the **h** in **herbaceous** and **herbivore**.
homage	Let's hear the **h**: **hahm'•ij**.
hors d'oeuvre	**awr'•durv'.** Please note that you do not pronounce the **s**. [The French do not pronounce the final **s** when they use the plural form.] "An appetizer."
hosiery	**hō'•zher•ee.**
hospitable	The accent is on the first syllable.
huge	**hyooj.** Let's hear the **h** at the beginning of the word.
human	**hyoo'•mun.** Always pronounce the **h**. Do not say *yoo*•mun.
humble	**hum'•bul.** That **h** is sounded.
humor	Sound the **h**: **hyoo•mur**.
hundred	**hun'•dred.** The last syllable rhymes with

Fred. Neither *hunnert* or *hunderd* is correct.

hypnotize   This word has many mispronunciations. It is not *hit'•nu•tīze* or *hip'•mu•tīze*. Say **hip'•nu•tīz.**

idea   Say this aloud. Did you add an **r** to the word? It is not *idear.*

Illinois   **Il•u•noi'.** "Noise" in this word bothers many people.

indict   **in•dīt'.** Rhymes with **light.** It means "to charge (usually with a crime)."

integral   **in'•te•grul.** It means "essential to completeness." Make sure that the **r** is in the right place: don't say *intregal.* It is not *in•teg'•ral,* either.

intermezzo   **in•tur•met'•sō.**

internecine   **in•tur•nes•ēn'.** Means "relating to a struggle within a group."

intravenous   **in•truh•vee'•nus.** Note that the word is not *in•ter'•venous.*

irrevocable   **i•rev'•u•ku•bl.** "Irreversible."

Italian   **I•tal'•yun.** Do not say *Eye•tal'•yun.*

italics   **ī•tal'•iks,** not *ī•tal'•iks.* It means "cursive print," such as the type used to designate incorrect pronunciations in this section.

jabot   **zhah•bō'.** "A cascade of frills down the front of a shirt."

jamb   **jam.** Do not sound the **b.** Posts or pieces of a door or window frame.

jewelry   **joo'•el•ree.** It has three syllables.

jocose   **jō•kōs'.** "Joking."

jocund   **jawk'•und.** "Merry," "of cheerful disposition."

jodhpurs   **jod'•purz,** not *jod'•furs.* The name derives from Jodhpur, a state of India.

junta   **hoon'•tah.** Give the **j** an **h** sound. It means "a group of military officers holding state power in a country after a *coup d'état.*"

just	Rhymes with **must**. Avoid the *jest* pronunciation.
juvenile	**joo′•vu•nul.** The last syllables does not rhyme with **mile**. It means "not yet adult."
karate	**ku•rah′•tee.** "A Japanese system of un-armed self-defense." The word literally means "empty-handed."
kibbutz	**ki•boŏts′.** The plural form is **kibbutzim: ki•boŏt•seem′.** A **kibbutz** is a "collective farm or settlement, usually in Israel."
kiln	**Kil** is still the preferred pronunciation.
kindergarten	**kin′•dur•gahr•tn.** It is not *kindergarden* or *kinny garden.*
kirsch	**kirsh.** Originally, "a colorless brandy made from the fermented juice of cherries."
knew	Pronounce **nyoo.**
knish	"Dough filled with meat or potato." Pronounce the **k.**
known	One syllable please: **nōn.**
lackadaisical	My favorite baseball manager is one of the many people who mispronounce this word. Pronounce it **lak•a•dā•zi•kul,** with no **s** in the second syllable.
lambaste	**lam•bāst′.** Slang. "To beat soundly, to scold severely."
larynx	**lar′•ingks.** It is not *lahr′•nicks.*
least	Pronounce the **t.**
length	**lengkth.** Avoid the *lenth* pronunciation.
liable	**lī′•u•bl.** Three syllables, in order not to confuse it with **libel.**
liaison	"A connecting link." It's pronounced **lee•ā′•zahn,** not *lee•u•zahn.*
library	**lī•brair•ee.** Please pronounce the **r** in the middle.
long-lived	**lawng•līvd′,** not *lawng•livd′.*
machinate	**mak′•i•nāt.** "To plot or to devise a plot."

maniacal	"Insane." Pronounce it **me•nī'•u•kul.**
manufacture	**man•yoo•fak'•chur.** Be sure to sound the **u** in the middle of this word.
marinade	**mar•u•nād'.**
marshmallow	The chances are good that if you spell it correctly, you will also say it correctly. It is **marsh'•mal•lō.**
mêl'ee	**mā'•lā.** "A confusing fracas."
menstruate	The word has three syllables: not *men'•strāte.*
mezzanine	**mez'•u•neen.**
milieu	**mē•lyoo'.** "Surroundings, environment."
miniature	**min'•ee•u•choor.** Please pronounce all four syllables. I still prefer the **t** sound for the last syllable, but most modern dictionaries give it the **ch** sound.
minutia	**mi•noo'•shee•u.** "A small or relatively unimportant detail." The plural of this word is **minutiae** and you pronounce it **mi•noo'•shee•ee.**
mischievous	**mis'•chi•vus.** Three syllables only.
mnemonics	**ni•mahn'•iks.** This is a plural noun, but it is used with a singular verb. It means "a system to improve or develop the memory."
modern	**mahd'•urn.** Please do not say *modren.*
motor	**mō•tur.** That is a **t** in the middle.
mousse	**moos.** "A light dessert."
Muenster	**mŏŏn'•stur.** A creamy, fermented cheese.
NASA	**nas'•a.** National Aeronautics and Space Administration. Do not mispronounce this as *Nassau,* the city.
notary public	Not *notory republic.*
nuclear	**noo'•klee•ur.** The late President Eisenhower said *noo'•kyu•lur,* but of course no one outranked him, so his pronunciation went uncorrected.

offertory The word has four syllables. Please note: There is no **a** in the middle of the word.

often **off'•n.** The **t** is silent.

once **wuhns.** This is a one-syllable word, without a **t.**

only **ōn'•lee.** Do not say *olny.*

ophthalmologist It means "eye doctor." It's **ahf•thal•mahl'•u•gist.**

orgy **or'•jee.** It means "unrestrained indulgence."

panache Say **pa•nash'.** It actually refers to a bunch of feathers or a plume. It also means "dash; verve."

particular **pahr•tik'•yoo•lur.** Be sure to sound all four syllables.

patina **pat'•u•nu.** "A shine or luster, or a coat of oxidation, as on brass or copper."

perfume **pur'•fyoom** is preferred.

permanent **pur'•mu•nent.** Do not reverse the **m** and the **n.**

persevere Don't add an extra **r** before the **v.**

perspiration **pur•spur•ā•shun.** The first syllable is **per,** not *pre.* A recent commercial presented a fashion designer who mispronounced this word.

petit **pet'•ee.** Used in law. It means "minor" or "petty."

petite **pu•teet'.** "Small, trim."

piano **pee•an'•o.** Avoid the **pī•a•no** pronunciation. Also avoid changing the final **o** to an **a.**

picture **pik'•chur.** Be sure to sound the **k** sound. *Pitch'•ur* is an unacceptable pronunciation for this word.

piquant **pee'•kunt.** "Having an agreeably pungent or tart taste; provocative."

piquante **pee•kahnt'.** Same meaning as above.

plagiarize	**plā'•ju•rīze.** Use a **j** in the middle, not a **g** as in **girl.** To use the ideas or writings of another as one's own.
poem	**po'•em.** Make that two syllables. No *pomes,* please.
poetry	**po'•e•tree.** Sound all three syllables.
poignant	**poin'•yent.** "Distressing."
poinsettia	**poin•set'•ee•u.**
porcine	**pawr'•sīn.** "Like a pig."
posthumous	**pahs'•choo•mus.** "Occurring or continuing after death."
précis	**prā•see'.** "A summary." Don't be confused by the accent.
prelude	The preferred pronunciation is **prel'•yood.**
pretzel	**prets'•l.** Be sure to begin with a **p.**
proboscis	**prō•bahs'•is.** A long snout, like an anteater's. Don't pronounce the **c.**
prohibition	**prō•i•bi'•shun.** The **h** is silent.
protein	You may say **pro'•teen** or **pro'•tee•in.**
proviso	**prō•vī•zō.** "A limiting clause in a contract."
pumpkin	**pump'•kin.**
quasi	**kwa'•zi.** "To some degree, almost, somewhat."
quay	**kee.** "A wharf."
quiche	**keesh.** "A custard, often with bacon and cheese, baked in an unsweetened pastry crust."
quiescent	**kwē•es'•unt.** "Still; silent."
quiet	**kwī•it.** This word has two syllables.
radiator	**rā'•dee•ā•tur.**
rapport	**ra•por'.** The **t** on the end of the word is silent.
ration	You may say **rash'•un** or **rā'•shun.**
recognize	The word is **rek'•ug•nīz.** Be sure the **g** in the middle is heard.
relapse	Most people use **ree•laps'** for the verb and

	ree'•laps for the noun, but **ree•laps'** is correct for both.
relator	The word you want is **Realtor.** Pronounce it **ree'•ul•tr** and not *ree•lä•tr.*Note that the **a** comes before the **l.** Refers to a real-estate agent affiliated with the National Association of Real Estate Boards.
relevant	**rel'•u•vent.** The **l** comes before the **v.**
remembrance	**ree•mem'•bruns.** Three syllables. Please do not say *ree•mem'•ber•ans.*
reservoir	**re'•zur•vwah.**
restaurant	**res'•tawr•ahnt.** The word has three syllables, not two.
résumé	"A summing up." Pronounce it **re'•zoo•mā** or **rā'•zoo•mā.**
Revelation	The last book in the New Testament is **Revelation** (without an s).
revenue	**re'•ven•yoo,** not *re'•ven•oo,*
rinse	**rins.** Do not say *wrench* for **rinse.**
robust	It means "strong, healthy," and it's pronounced **ro•bust'.**
roof	Pronounce it **roof** not *ruf.*
root beer	The **root** rhymes with **boot,** not *book.*
rosé	**rō•zā'.** "A wine that is suitable for either white or dark meat; it is pink in color."
route	Pronounce either **root** or **rowt.** The pronunciation **root** is given first in most dictionaries.
saboteur	**sab•u•ter'.**
sacrilegious	**sak•ru•lee'•jus.** "Irreverent."
sadism	**sā'diz' um.**
sauterne	**sō•tairn'.** "A white table wine."
schism	**siz'•em.** "A separation."
scion	**si'•en.** "A descendant or heir."
sexual	**sek'•shoo•ul.** Not *seks'•yoo ul.*
sherbet	**sher'•bit.** Note that it is not *sherbert.*
shown	**shōn.** One syllable.

similar	**sim′•i•ler.** "Resembling." Do not pronounce it *sim′•yoo-ler.*
sink	As it's spelled—not *zink.*
soiree	**swah•rā′.** "A party."
solder	**sahd′•r.** The **l** is silent.
soprano	Be sure to sound an **o** at the end of the word (it does not end with **a).**
sotto voce	**sawt′•ō•vō•chee.** "Very softly; in an undertone."
species	**spee′•sheez.**
strength	**strengkth.** Do not say *strenth.*
suite	Pronounce it **sweet.** It means "a succession of related things; a series of connected rooms; a matched set of furniture." (Please note: you may have a **suit (soot)** of clothes, but you do not have a *suit* of furniture.)
surprise	**sur•prīz′.** Note that the pronunciation is not *suh′•prīz.*
table d'hôte	**taw′•blu•dōt** (literally, "table of the host"). "Meal of the house served at a fixed price."
tarot	**ta•rō′.**
temperamental	This word has five syllables. Be sure to sound both the **er** and the **a** syllables in the middle of the word.
temperature	**tem′•pur•u•chur.** Pronounce all four syllables.
theater	**thee′•u•tur.** Do not say *thee•ā′•tur.*
thorough	**thur′•ō.** Never put an **l** in this word (making it *thorul).*
tired	**tīrd.**
toward	**Tord** is the preferred pronunciation in the United States.
tract	Do not say *tract* when you mean **track.**
Tuesday	It is **tyooz′•dā,** say the purists; **tooz′•dā** now appears in many dictionaries.

umbrella	**um•brel′•u.**
undoubtedly	**un•dau′•ted•lee.** Do not pronounce the **b** in **doubt.**
valet	**val′•et.**
vapid	**vap′•id.** "Tasteless, dull."
vaudeville	**vōd′•vil.**
vehement	**vee′•u•ment.** The **h** remains silent.
veldt	The word is sometimes spelled **veld.** It is pronounced **felt** or **veld.**
veterinarian	**vet•ur•u•nar′•ee•un.** There are six syllables. The word *vet* is not pleasing to most veterinarians.
via	Either **vī′•u** or **vee′•u** is correct. (The meaning is usually restricted to "by way of"; "by means of" is not an accepted meaning.)
viaduct	**vī′•u•dukt.** Note that it is not *vī′•u•dahk.*
vice versa	You may say **vī′•see•vur′•su** OR **vīs′•vur′•su.** I no longer laugh inwardly when I hear that first pronunciation. That's the way many experts say it.
vichyssoise	**vee′•shee•swahz.** Pronounce the final **s** as a **z.**
victuals	**vit′•ls.** "Food."
vignette	**vin•yet′.** "Ornamental design; a picture; a short literary composition."
virago	**vi•rā′•gō.** "A bad-tempered woman."
voyeur	**vwah•yur′.** A person who obtains gratification by looking at sexual objects or scenes.
wash	Please do not say *wawrsh.* There is no **r** in the word.
Washington	The first syllable does not have an **r** in it.
Westminster	No *minister* here, please.
whale	There is an **h** in the word. It is pronounced **hwāl,** and rhymes with **mail.**
what	**hwaht.** Sound the **h.**

when	**hwen.** Sound the **h.**
where	**hwair.** Sound the **h.** And the word rhymes with **care**, not *car.*
which	**hwich.** Sound the **h.**
while	**hwīl.** Sound the **h.**
white	**hwīt.** Sound the **h.**
with	Pronounce the **th** as you do in father.
wrestle	Not *ras'•sel,* but **res' ul.**
Xavier	**Zā'•vee•ur.**
yellow	Avoid the *yella* pronunciation.
zoology	**zō•ahl'•u•jee.** The first syllable rhymes with **go** rather than with *to.*

4

BEYOND THE BASICS

For last year's words belong to last year's language
And next year's words await another voice.

—T. S. ELIOT
Little Gidding

The words I want to talk about in this section touch on the subtleties of language. Most are neither right nor wrong. But they do leave traces of where you've been and who you've been.

• They reveal the extent of your education—in some instances, the extent of your parents' educations.
• They tell whether you're young or old, contemporary or old-fashioned.
• They tell whether you're observant.
• They tell whether you've travelled.
• And they have a lot to do with where you're going and who you're going to be.

I credit Vance Packard's *The Status Seekers* with my idea for a collection of up-scale and down-scale words. But I couldn't stop with just snob words. For the more I studied the effect of word choice, the more I realized that words describe the person using them.

There are new words, dated words, old words, young words, rich words and poor words. There are political words too—words that tag the speaker as liberal or conservative. An aura often hovers about a word—a connotation that you won't find explained in any dictionary. This aura influences the listener's response to the speaker.

I've worked on my list of up-scale and down-scale words for years. Perhaps you saw them in a chapter called "Help for 'hear'-ache" in *Martin's Magic Formula for Getting the Right Job*. In the book, I called them "plus and minus words" because the reflection they cast on the speaker is shaped by more than mere station in life. Writing on this theme of words working *for* or *against* the speaker, I also referred to "plus and minus words" in articles I did for *Aloft* and *Writer's Digest* magazines. The chances are even greater that you saw William Safire's collection of such words in recent *On Language* columns in *The New York Times*.

I can tell you I was elated over a particular column; Mr. Safire called it "Caste Party." In it, he referred to *my* list— bless him—and then included some of my words with his.

I was even more elated when he gave me permission to use his words as well as his headings in this chapter. His headings are more to the mark than mine. He refers to "Out-of-it" words and "On-top-of-it" words. Following the principle that one should adopt apt words and phrases, I shall do just that. Here then, you have my latest and greatest collection of "Out-of-it" and "On-top-of-it" terms.

Do remember as you look at this list that I spend a lot of my life as a columnist; the reporting instinct is strong. I'm following it here. I am *reporting* on the listener's response to words. I am not responsible for that response.

Out-of-it Words	**On-top-of-it Words**
a hold of	**reach**
air corps (Use to refer to the old Air Corps only.)	**air force**
bathing suit	**swimsuit**

Out-of-it Words	On-top-of-it Words
bathrobe (for a woman)	hostess gown or robe
bawl out	scold, reprimand
better half	wife, husband
blackboard	chalkboard (Black is no longer the prevailing color of chalkboards.)
bride and groom	bride and bridegroom
British citizen	British subject
bushes	shrubs
butcher	meat cutter
cake of soap	bar of soap
car wreck	car accident
chaise lounge	chaise longue, pronounced shāz long (If you learn to spell longue, you'll have no more trouble with this.)
Chief Justice of the Supreme Court	Chief Justice of the United States
Chinaman	Chinese, someone from China
claim	say
clap	applaud
cleaning woman	domestic
coffeepot	coffee maker
coffee table	cocktail table
colored, Negro	Black, Afro-American
costume jewelry	fashion jewelry
cuss	curse
deaf and dumb	deaf, hearing-impaired (Most persons who have hearing impairments do speak.)
dig an oil well	drill an oil well
dishrag	dishcloth
dish towel	tea towel
divorced	newly single
drapes	draperies
drugstore	pharmacy
eats	food

Out-of-it Words	On-top-of-it Words
electric (as *The electric is off.*)	electricity or electric power
ex-husband	former husband
fireman	firefighter
fish tank	aquarium
folks	parents, family, relatives
funnies	comics
gal or girl (for an adult female)	woman
galoshes	boots, rubbers, overshoes
girlfriend, boyfriend	friend
graduated	was graduated from
graveyard	cemetery, memorial park
grip	bag, baggage, suitcase
gym (in reference to health club)	spa
hair (One sometimes refers to hair and incorrectly says, *shampoo them?*)	hair—Shampoo it, not *them,* is correct.
half-a-dollar	fifty cents
heavyset	overweight
home (as an edifice)	house
hopefully	I hope
icebox	refrigerator
idiot	developmentally disadvantaged
lame	crippled, handicapped, disabled
machine (for automobile)	automobile, car
maiden name	birth name
manpower	human energy, human power
material, goods	fabric
middle-age	midlife
the missus, the mister	my wife or Mrs. Martin or Phyllis; my husband or Mr. Martin or Bruce

Out-of-it Words	On-top-of-it Words
movies	films
of a night	at night
out loud	aloud
passed away	died
piano player	pianist
picture (when you mean painting)	painting
pocketbook	handbag
porch	deck
postman	mail carrier
present	gift
press conference	news conference (Use press conference only if conference is limited to members of the press.)
Princess Diana	The word from Buckingham Palace is that she should be referred to as The Princess of Wales.
railroad station	train station
Reverend or Rev. Campbell	the Rev. Mr. (or Dr.) Campbell
rouge	blusher
row house	town house
Sahara Desert	Sahara (Sahara means "desert" so you don't need to repeat the word.)
sassy	saucy
shelves	wall system
shot (as in medicine)	injection
Sierra Mountains	Sierras (*Mountains* is inherent in Sierras, of Spanish derivation, so you don't need to say *mountains* twice.)
Smithsonian Institute	Smithsonian Institution
sneakers	running shoes
socket	fixture
soprano singer	soprano (It is all right to refer to a soprano saxophone.)

Out-of-it Words	On-top-of-it Words
square	**block**
stewardess	**flight attendant**
stockings	**hose, hosiery**
switchboard	**console**
tease (as hair)	**back comb**
They got married.	**They were married.**
trunks	**shorts**
tux	**black tie**
undertaker	**funeral director**
unwed mother	**single mother**
vet	**veterinarian,** or **doctor of veterinary medicine**
wash rag	**washcloth**
watch	**timepiece**
Wimpleton	**Wimbledon,** pronounced **wim′•b′l•dan** (if you are referring to the site of the famous tennis matches).
women's lib	**women's liberation**
yeah	**yes**

Want a few more hints on plus and minus words? Here's a column from Ann Landers that contains several new examples:

Phyllis Martin has a few words for Ann Landers

DEAR ANN LANDERS: Why all the fuss because a TV news commentator says, "Febyooary," when all around us we hear "cold slaw," "sherbert," "realtor," and "irregardless"—to mention just a few nerve grinders? The abuse of the English language has become so commonplace that our ears will soon be accustomed to non-words and atrocious usage. Please do your bit by printing this, Ann. I'm signing myself—In Need Of Earmuffs.

DEAR EAR: Funny you should write today. I just read a book by Phyllis Martin, a Cincinnati job counselor and business consultant and a columnist for the Cincinnati Post. It's "Word Watcher's Handbook" (McKay, publisher, a paperback, $3.95). While the author didn't say anything about "cold slaw," "sherbert," or "realtor," "irregardless" was listed right up with words that are obsolete.

Phyllis also tells us it is better to say "over" than "overly." She asks that we avoid "over with." Just plain "over" will do.

"Personal friend" is one word too many. "Friend" is enough. The same goes for "personal opinion." If it's your opinion, it's personal.

Anyone who says "needless to say" is saying too much. If it was needless, you wouldn't be saying it.

"Muchly" was O.K. a few hundred years ago but it's a bit much now.

Don't say "enthused" when you mean "enthusiastic."

The word is "famous," not "famed."

"Fantastic" is probably one of the most overworked words of our time. Get out of the rut and look up synonyms. You will be surprised to discover what the word fantastic really means.

"Gentlemen"—not "gent," please.

"Heartrendering" is not a word. It's "heartrending." Fat is rendered, not hearts.

"At this point in time" and "frame of reference" are children of Watergate and everybody is sick to death of them.

"Gross" is overused, especially by the young. Try "vulgar" or "coarse."

The phrase "I don't think" is another dud. How can you express an opinion if you don't think? Say instead, "I think not."

"Hisself" is not a word. "Himself" is what you are after.

"Learning experience" doesn't mean anything. Either you learn from experience or you don't.

Not all "h's" should be dropped, as in "honorable." Don't say "umble," say "humble."

"Unbeknownst" is a pompous substitute for the simple word "unknown." Don't be stuffy.

Phrases that grate from overuse are, "You can say that again"—"See what I mean"—"Due to the fact"—"How about that?" (You can also add to the list, "Have a nice day," and "Is it hot enough for you?")

Some of the most often mispronounced words are "knew"—it's not "noo," it's "nyoo." "Jewelry" is not "jool-ry." It's "jew-el-ree"—THREE syllables. "Prohibition" is "PRO-I-BI-SHUN." THE "h" is silent.

How many of you readers learned something today? I did. The book is fantastic—er —uh—I mean I'm enthused—pardon me—enthusiastic about it.

BRAND NAMES

Many manufacturers have lost their trademarks as a result of indiscriminate use of brand names. Limit your use of the following names to those times when you refer to the product or manufacturer in question.

Band-Aid	adhesive bandage
Clorox	bleach
Coca-Cola	cola
Coke (Coke is a registered name for Coca-Cola.)	cola
Davenport (This word is now considered old fashioned.)	sofa, divan
Fiberglas	fiber glass
Formica *	laminated plastic
Frigidaire	refrigerator
IBM	computer
Jell-O	gelatin
Kleenex	facial tissue
Magic Marker	felt-tipped pen
Scotch tape	cellophane † tape or transparent tape
Teleprompter	prompting device
Thermos	vacuum bottle
Vaseline	petroleum jelly
Xerox	copier

---

* The manufacturers of Formica almost lost exclusive rights to their famous trademark because people grew careless and referred to all laminated plastic as Formica. It took Congressional action to save the word. See why manufacturers wince when you misuse their trademarks?

† The word cellophane was originally Cellophane, a trademark. The manufacturer lost exclusive rights to the word because people used it as a generic term.

AN AWARENESS TEST

This test has nothing to do with rules governing our use of words. It is designed to remind us that it takes a lot of listening and looking if our lines of communication are going to be free of blockages.

Scoring: Give yourself ten points for each correct answer.

1. How would you refer to the bride of the Prince of Wales?
   a. Princess Diana
   b. The Princess of Wales
2. Which is preferred?
   a. *Oxfordians* are proud of their university.
   b. *Oxonians* are proud of their university.
3. Does this sentence sound all right to you? "We were pleased to hear that San Franciscans are riding trolley cars again."
4. If I were quoting the poet Thomas Gray, would I say,
   a. "all that glisters" is not gold, *or*
   b. "all that glistens" is not gold?
5. Is this an accurate quotation?
   "Money is the root of all evil"?
6. What is wrong with this sentence?
   "She is going to premiere in his play."
7. What is wrong with this statement?
   "I second the nomination."
8. Is a moderator correct in asking for a motion to adjourn?
9. Which is correct?
   a. chaise longue
   b. chaise lounge
10. I recently wrote to The Proctor & Gamble Company. Did I spell the name correctly?

Key:

1. The word from Buckingham Palace is that she should be referred to as **The Princess of Wales**.
2. **Oxonian** is preferred.
3. As in the song, it's "little **cable** cars climb halfway to the stars."
4. The actual quotation is:
   "Not all that tempts your wand'ring eyes
   And heedless hearts, is lawful prize;
   Nor all, that glist**ers**, gold."

   Yes, I was surprised too.
   Thanks for setting me straight, Jim Fallon.
5. The correct quotation—from the Bible—is:
   "The **love of** money is the root of all evil."—I Timothy 6:10
6. The word **premiere** is not a verb. It is a noun.
7. It is not necessary for anyone to second a nomination. Furthermore, a moderator should not ask for a second to a nomination. Reason? It could cause embarrassment to the nominee if a second were not forthcoming.
8. No. When the business for which the meeting was called has been transacted, the moderator may declare the meeting adjourned.
9. It is **chaise longue**, pronounced **shāz long.**
10. No. **Procter** is spelled with **er** at the end. It is not Proc*tor*.

Rate Yourself:

100	You rub everyone the right way. Congratulations.
80–90	You are very astute.
60–70	You are above average in awareness.
40–50	You need to grab your share of listening time.

0-30   You will need to increase the amount of reading
         you do, as well as the amount of listening.

Note: The truly observant reader will have noted the answers
to numbers 1 and 9 in the word list on pages 76–80 and
thereby raised the awareness score.

5

REVIEWING FOREIGN MENU TERMS

I am indebted to Marjabelle Young Stewart and Marian Faux for permitting me to include this chapter for you. It was because I referred to Mrs. Stewart's and Ms. Faux's book, *Executive Etiquette* in a television "job spot" (for WKRC-TV, Cincinnati) that I learned that they and I have the same editor, Barbara Anderson.

I would like to show you more of the *Executive Etiquette* material but this is *my* book. Now that you know St. Martin's Press is the publisher, you can acquire your own copy of *Executive Etiquette.* You'll like Marjabelle Stewart's latest, *Book of Modern Table Manners,* too.

I am also indebted to Library Larousse for permission to reprint the French pronunciation key from the *Larousse French/English-English/French Modern Dictionary.*

REVIEWING FOREIGN MENU TERMS

Familiarity with some foreign words and expressions is the mark of an educated person, to say nothing of the fact that it will help you order food in a French restaurant, find the right train in Germany, and read some scholarly works. The most commonly used foreign words and phrases come from French, German, and Latin.

A word of warning here: knowledge of foreign words and expressions should be put to discreet use. Sprinkling one's

CONSONANTS

SYMBOLS	KEY WORDS
[b]	bas [bɑ]
[d]	dame [dam]
[dʒ]	djinn [dʒin], bridge [bridʒ]
[f]	fin [fɛ̃], aphte [aft]
[g]	gris [gri], guerre [gɛːr], ghetto [gɛto], aggraver [agrave], second [səgɔ̃]
[gn]	gnome [gnom]
[ɲ]	pagne [paɲ]
[gw]	lingual [lɛ̃gwal]
[gɥ]	linguiste [lɛ̃gɥist]
[gz]	exempt [egzɑ̃], eczéma [egzema]
[ʒ]	jaspe [ʒasp], genêt [ʒənɛ], geai [ʒɛ]
[*]	héros [*ero]
[k]	caduc [kadyk], kaki [kaki], khédive [kəːdiːv], úahø [ckø], ecchymose [ɛkimoːz], queue [kø], becqueter [bɛkte]
[ks]	équinoxe [ekinɔks], coccyx [kɔksis]
[kw]	quartz [kwarts]
[l]	lent [lɑ̃], bacille [basil]
[m]	mime [mim], gemme [ʒɛm]
[n]	nef [nɛf], bonne [bɔn], automne [otɔn]
[p]	part [par], appel [apɛl]
[r]	roi [rwa], terre [tɛːr], arrhes [aːr]
[s]	lis, lice [lis], ceci [səsi], scie [si], facétie [fasesi], garçon [garsɔ̃]
[ʃ]	chat [ʃa], schisme [ʃism], shampooing [ʃɑ̃pwɛ̃]
[sk]	scandale [skɑ̃dal], ski [ski], schizophrène [skizɔfrɛn]
[skw]	squame [skwam]
[t]	taupe [toːp], thé [te], sotte [sɔt]
[tʃ]	tchèque [tʃɛk]
[v]	vent [vɑ̃], wagon [vagɔ̃]
[z]	zèle [zɛːl], rose [roːz]

VOWELS

SYMBOLS	KEY WORDS
[a]	bague [bag], tabac [taba], surah [syra], drap [dra], plat [pla], orgeat [orʒa], femme [fam]
[aː]	tard [taːr]
[ɑ]	ras, raz [rɑ], bât [bɑ]
[ɑː]	sable [sɑːbl], âge [ɑʒ]
[e]	été [ete], pied [pje], bouchée [buʃe], crier [krije], volontiers [vɔlɔ̃tje], nez [ne]
[ɛ]	freiner [frɛne], legs [lɛg], sept [sɛt], abcès [absɛ], est [ɛ], archet [arʃɛ], rets [rɛ], bey [bɛ], vrai [vrɛ], laid, lait [lɛ], sagaie [sagɛ], rabais [rabɛ], faix [fɛ]
[ɛː]	treize [trɛːz], hêtre [*ɛːtr], paire [pɛːr], mère [mɛːr]
[i]	ni, nid [ni], lubie [lybi], fusil [fyzi], habit [abi], pris, prix [pri], riz [ri], jury [ʒyri], abbaye [abɛi], pays [pei]
[iː]	rire [riːr], abîme [abiːm], lyre [liːr]
[o]	franco [frɑ̃ko], accroc [akro], galop [galo], chaos [kao], sabot [sabo], au, eau, aulx [o], chaud, chaux [ʃo], haut [*o]
[oː]	aube [oːb], heaume [*oːm], rose [roːz], côte [koːt]
[ɔ]	tonne [tɔn], oignon [ɔɲɔ̃]
[ɔː]	éloge [elɔːʒ], mors [mɔːr]
[ø]	bleu [blø], queue [kø], nœud [nø], émeut [emø], œufs, eux [ø]
[øː]	veule [vøːl], jeûne [ʒøːn]
[œ]	seul [sœl], œuf [œf], cueillir [kœjiːr]
[œː]	peur [pœːr], œuvre [œːvr]
[u]	cou, coud, coût, coup [ku], boue, bout [bu], joug [ʒu], août [u], pouls [pu], goût [gu], houx [*u], remous [rəmu], saoul, sou, sous [su]
[uː]	rouge [ruːʒ], bourg [buːr]
[y]	cru, crû, crue [kry], rude [ryd], jus [ʒy], début [deby], flux [fly], ciguë [sigy], eu [y]
[yː]	ruse [ryːz], usure [yzyːr], bûche [byːʃ], gageure [gaʒyːr]
[ə]	le [lə], regard [rəgaːr], benêt [bənɛ]

SEMI-VOWELS

SYMBOLS	KEY WORDS
[j]	p*ie*u [pjø], plé*i*ade [plejad], jo*y*eux [ʒwajø], gri*ll*on [grijɔ̃], mai*ll*on [majɔ̃]
[w]	*w*allon [walɔ̃], *ou*ate [wat], q*u*adruple [kwadrypl], jag*u*ar [ʒagwa:r] (cf. [kw], [gw])

CLUSTERS

SYMBOLS	KEY WORDS
[i:j]	f*ille* [fi:j]
[œj]	*œille*t [œjɛ], cu*eille*tte [kœjɛt]
[œ:j]	s*euil* [sœ:j], *œil* [œ:j]
[øj]	f*euille*t [føjɛ]
[ø:j]	f*euille* [fø:j]

CLUSTERS
SEMI-VOWELS AND VOWELS

SYMBOLS	KEY WORDS
[wa]	l*oi* [lwa], fr*oid* [frwa], p*oid*s [pwa], pr*oie* [prwa], f*ois* [fwa], d*oig*t, d*oit* [dwa], ch*oix* [ʃwa], *ou*ate [wat]
[wa:]	l*oir* [lwa:r]
[ɥi]	n*uit* [nɥi], m*uid* [mɥi], pl*uie* [plɥi], b*uis* [bɥi], fr*uit* [frɥi], p*uy* [pɥi]
[ɥe]	arg*uer* [argɥe]
[a:j]	b*ail* [ba:j], cob*aye* [kɔba:j], m*aille* [ma:j]
[ɑ:j]	b*âille*r [bɑ:je]
[ɛj]	grass*ey*er [grasɛje], bal*ay*er [balɛje]
[ɛ:j]	sol*eil* [sɔlɛ:j], v*eille* [vɛ:j], p*aye* [pɛ:j], ass*eye* [asɛ:j]
[ij]	p*illage* [pija:ʒ]

NASALS

SYMBOLS	KEY WORDS
[ɑ̃]	c*am*per [kɑ̃pe], anc*ien* [ɑ̃sjɛ̃], b*anc* [bɑ̃], march*and* [marʃɑ̃], s*ang* [sɑ̃], cé*ans* [seɑ̃], pa*on* [pɑ̃], trembl*ant* [trɑ̃blɑ̃], f*end* [fɑ̃], *en*cens [ɑ̃sɑ̃], tourm*ent* [turmɑ̃], *em*pan [ɑ̃pɑ̃], t*em*ps [tɑ̃], exe*mp*t [egzɑ̃]
[ɑ̃:]	*ang*e [ɑ̃:ʒ], *am*ple [ɑ̃:pl], *en*cre [ɑ̃:kr], s*em*ble [sɑ̃:bl]
[ɛ̃]	*in*stinct [ɛ̃stɛ̃], v*ingt*, v*in*, v*ain*, v*ainc* [vɛ̃], qu*int* [kɛ̃], *im*pie [ɛ̃pi], th*ym*, t*ain* [tɛ̃], s*aint*, s*eing*, c*eint* [sɛ̃], ess*aim* [esɛ̃], ex*amen* [egzamɛ̃], appe*ndi*ce [apɛ̃dis], v*iens* [vjɛ̃]
[ɛ̃:]	l*inge* [lɛ̃:ʒ], cr*ainte* [krɛ̃:t], g*eindre* [ʒɛ̃:dr]
[ɔ̃]	n*on*, n*om* [nɔ̃], pl*omb* [plɔ̃], r*omps*, r*ond* [rɔ̃], pr*ompt* [prɔ̃], j*onc* [ʒɔ̃], b*ond* [bɔ̃], l*ong* [lɔ̃], rép*ons* [repɔ̃], m*ont* [mɔ̃], f*onts* [fɔ̃], lumb*ago* [lɔ̃bago]
[ɔ̃:]	*onde* [ɔ̃:d], *ombre* [ɔ̃:br], j*ungle* [ʒɔ̃:gl]
[œ̃]	al*un* [alœ̃], parf*um* [parfœ̃], j*eun* [ʒœ̃], empr*unt* [ɑ̃prœ̃]
[œ̃:]	déf*unte* [defœ̃:t], h*umble* [œ̃:bl]

conversation with foreign words does not show that one is well-travelled; it indicates that one is showing off. A parallel can perhaps be drawn between knowing and using foreign expressions and knowing how to play a bagpipe: A gentleman, it has been said, is someone who knows how to play the instrument but refrains from actually doing so.

The best way to feel secure in using foreign expressions is to hear someone else speak them, so don't be shy about asking an expert speaker in a language how to say something or taking a few language lessons. There are also many good books on foreign grammar and speaking that will help you become familiar with useful expressions.

The foreign terms that Americans are most likely to encounter are those found on menus in French restaurants. Here is a list of the most commonly used expressions:

agneau [añô]	lamb
ull [ay]	garlic
à la [a] [la]	in the style of
amandine [amãdin]	made with almonds; often used in preparing fish fillets
ananas [ananâ]	pineapple
anchois [ãʃwa]	anchovy
anglaise, à la [ãglɛ:z]	cooked in either water or stock
artichauts [artiʃo]	artichokes
artichauts à la vinaigrette [vinɛgrɛt]	artichokes in olive oil and garlic
asperges [aspɛrʒ]	asparagus
assiette anglaise [asjɛt]	assortment of cold cuts
aubergine [oberʒi:n]	eggplant
au jus [o] [ʒy]	in its own juice
au lait [lɛ]	with milk
avocat [avɔka]	avocado
baba au rhum [baba] [rɔm]	cake soaked in rum after it has been baked
banane [banan]	banana

basilic [bazilik]	basil
béarnaise [bearnez]	thick sauce made with shallots, tarragon, thyme, bay leaf, vinegar, white wine and egg yolks, served with grilled or sautéed meat or grilled fish
béchamel [beʃamɛ:l]	sauce of milk thickened with butter and flour
beurre d'ail [bœ:r] [a:j]	garlic butter
beurre noir [nwa:r]	brown butter served on eggs, fish, or vegetables
bière [bjɛ:r]	beer
biscuits [biskyi]	cookies
bisque [bisk]	soup, usually made of puréed shellfish
blanquette de veau [blãkɛt] [vo]	veal stewed in a cream sauce
boeuf [boef]	beef
boeuf bourguignon [burgiɲɔ̃]	braised beef prepared in the style of Burgundy (with small glazed onions, mushrooms and red wine)
boeuf rôti [roti]	roast beef
bombe glacée [bɔ̃:b] [glase]	ice cream dessert
bon bon [bɔ̃]	candy
bonne femme, à la [bɔn] [fam]	cooked with bacon, onions, potatoes and a thick brown gravy
bordelaise [bɔrdəlɛz]	brown sauce made with wine and bone marrow
boudin [bu dɛ̃]	blood sausage
bouillabaisse [bujabɛs]	fish chowder from French Riviera; made with fish, olive oil, tomatoes, and saffron with water or bouillon
bouilli [bu ji]	boiled
braisée [brɛ ze]	braised
brioche [bri jɔʃ]	a kind of French bread
brochette [brɔ ʃɛt]	a skewer; anything cooked on a skewer may be called a *brochette*

brocoli [brɔkɔli]	broccoli
brouillé [bruje]	scrambled
café glacé [kafe glase]	ice cream with coffee flavoring
calmar [kal mar]	squid
canapé [kanape]	a small round of bread, topped with various spreads and used as an appetizer
canard [ka nar]	duck
canard à l'orange [ɔrã:ʒ]	duck in orange sauce
caneton [kantɔ̃]	duckling
câpres, sauce aux [kɑ:pr]	caper sauce, used most often on lamb
carbonnade à la flamande [karbɔ̃nad]	beef cooked with beer
carottes [karɔt]	carrots
cassoulet [kasule]	stew made with white beans and pork
cervelles [sɛrvɛl]	brains
champignons [ʃãpiɲɔ̃]	mushrooms
châteaubriand [ʃɑtobrijã]	cut of beef, grilled and served with vegetables cut in strips and with a *béarnaise* sauce
choix [ʃwa]	choice
choux de bruxelles [ʃu] [brysɛl]	Brussels sprouts
ciboulette [sibulɛt]	chives
citron [sitrɔ̃]	lemon
coeurs d'artichaut [kœr] [artiʃo]	artichoke hearts
compote de fruits [kɔ̃pɔt] [fryi]	stewed, mixed fruit (fresh or dried), served cold
consommé [kɔ̃sɔme]	meat stock that has been enriched, concentrated, and clarified
coq au vin [kɔk] [o] [vɛ̃]	chicken in a red wine sauce with mushrooms, garlic, small onions, and diced pork
coquillages [kɔkijaʒ]	shellfish

coquilles St. Jacques [kɔki]	scallops
cornichon [kɔrniʃɔ̃]	type of small pickle, served with pâté and other dishes
côte de boeuf grillé [kot] [bœf] [grije]	grilled beef rib
côte de veau [vo]	veal chop
courgette [kurzet]	zucchini
crabe [kra:b]	crab
crème [krɛm]	custard or cream
crème brûlée [bryle]	a rich dessert pudding made with vanilla and cream, which is lightly coated with sugar, placed under the broiler, and then cooled for two to three hours before serving
crème caramel [karamɛl]	custard with a burnt sugar flavor
crème Chantilly [ʃɑ̃tji]	whipped cream
crêpes [krɛ:p]	thin pancakes
crêpes Suzette	thin dessert pancakes topped with a sauce made with curaçao and the juice of mandarin oranges, usually served flaming
crevettes [krəvɛt]	shrimp
croissant [krwasɑ̃]	crescent-shaped roll made with a puff pastry or yeast dough; most often served at breakfast
croque madame [krɔk]	chicken and cheese sandwich, grilled
croque monsieur [məsjø]	ham and cheese sandwich, fried
croûtons [krutɔ̃]	bread that has been diced and sautéed in butter; used in soup and on salads
crudités [krydite]	raw vegetables served as an appetizer
cuisses de grenouilles [kyis] [grənu:j]	frogs' legs
daube [do:b]	chunks of meat stewed with vegetables

demiglace [dəmiglas]	a thick, brown sauce
demitasse [dəmitɑːse]	strong, black coffee served in a small cup
diable, sauce à la [djaːbl]	spicy sauce of white wine, vinegar, shallots, and pepper
dinde [dɛ̃ːd]	turkey
dolmas [dɔlmɑ]	stuffing wrapped in a vine leaf
duglère, à la [dygler]	with a cream sauce made with wine and tomatoes, served with fish
échalotte [eʃalɔt]	shallot
écrevisse [ekrəvis]	crawfish
en croûte [krut]	baked in a pastry crust
entrecôte [ãtrəkoːt]	translates as "between the ribs"; steak cut from between two ribs of beef, usually grilled or fried
entrecôte marchand de vin [marʃã]	steak cooked with red wine and shallots
épinards [epɪnaːr]	spinach
escalopes de veau [ɛskalɔp]	thin, boneless slices of veal
escalopes de veau cordon bleu [kɔrdɔ̃ blø]	thin, boneless slices of veal with ham and cheese
escargots [ɛskargo]	snails
farci [farsi]	stuffed
filet de boeuf [filɛ]	tenderloin
filet mignon [miɲɔ̃]	small, choice cut of beef prepared by grilling or sautéeing
flambé [flãbe]	describes a dish that has been ignited after being doused in a liqueur
florentine, à la [flɔrentin]	foods cooked in this style (usually eggs or fish) are put on spinach, covered with mornay sauce, and sprinkled with cheese
foie [fwa]	liver
foie gras [grɑ]	the livers of fattened geese and ducks
fraises [frɛːz]	strawberries

framboises [frãbwa:z]	raspberries
frappé [frape]	chilled
frites [frit]	french fries
fromage [frɔma:ʒ]	cheese
fruits de mer [fryi] [mɛr]	seafood
garni [garni]	garnished or decorated
gâteau [gɑto]	cake
gigot d'agneau [ʒigo] [aɲo]	leg of lamb
glace [glas]	ice cream
gratin, au [gratẽ]	prepared with a topping of toasted breadcrumbs; usually includes grated cheese
hareng [arã]	herring
haricots [ariko]	beans
herbe [ɛrb]	herb
hollandaise [ɔlãdɛ:z]	sauce made with egg yolks and butter; served over vegetables and fish
homard [ɔma:r]	lobster
hors d'oeuvre [ɔ:r] [œ:vr]	appetizers, hot or cold
huîtres [yi:tr]	oysters
jambon fumé [ʒãbɔ̃] [fyme]	smoked ham
jardinière, à la [ʒardinjɛ:r]	fresh vegetables, served with roast, stewed, or braised meat and poultry
julienne [ʒyljɛn]	meat or vegetables cut into thin strips
lait [lɛ]	milk
laitue [lɛty]	lettuce
lapin [lapẽ]	rabbit
légumes [legym]	vegetables
lyonnaise [liɔ̃nez]	prepared with onions
macédoine [masedwan]	fruit or vegetables, diced and then mixed
madeleine [madlɛn]	sweet made from flour, butter, eggs, and sugar baked in shell-like molds

madère, sauce au [madɛ:r]	sauce made with Madeira wine
madrilène [madrilɛn]	clear chicken soup with tomato; served chilled
maison [mɛzɔ̃]	a term applied only to recipes that are exclusive to the restaurant's owner or chef but usually used more loosely to mean in the style of the restaurant
marchands de vin, sauce [marʃɑ̃]	brown sauce of butter and red wine
maître d'hotel [mɛ:tr] [otɛl]	headwaiter
médaillon [medajɔ̃]	food cut into a round or oval shape
menthe [mɑ̃:t]	mint
meunière [mønjɛ:r]	method of preparing fish; the fish is first seasoned, floured, and fried in butter, then served with lemon juice, parsley, and melted butter
mornay [mɔrnɛ]	white sauce with cheese added
moules [mul]	mussels
mousse [mus]	a light, airy dish made with cream and eggs; may be of fish, chicken, fruits, or chocolate; served hot or cold
moutarde [mutard]	mustard
nature [naty:r]	plain; without trim; in its natural state
niçoise, à la [niswaz]	a dish cooled in the style of Nice, often prepared with tomatoes, zucchini, garlic, potatoes, green beans, olives, garlic capers and anchovies
nouilles [nu:j]	noodles
oeuf [œf]	egg
oeufs à la Russe [rys]	hard-boiled eggs with a mayonnaise sauce of chives, onion, and a dash of tabasco
oeufs bénédictine	in most American restaurants this

[benediktin]	refers to an egg and ham on an English muffin with hollandaise sauce and possibly a slice of truffle
oignon [ɔɲɔ̃]	onion
omelette [ɔmlɛt]	omelet; an egg dish
omelette aux fines herbes [fi:n]	omelet made with parsley, tarragon, and chives or another combination of herbs
pain [pɛ̃]	bread
palourdes [palurd]	clams
papillote, en [papijɔt]	steamed, enclosed in a sheet of parchment
parfait [parfɛ]	an iced dessert
pâté [pɑte]	any dish of ground meat or fish baked in a mold that has been lined with strips of fat
pâté maison [mɛzɔ̃]	a pâté unique to a particular restaurant
pâtisseries [pɑtisri]	pastries
pêche [pɛ:ʃ]	peach
pêches melba	peaches that have been steeped in vanilla-flavored syrup, served over vanilla ice cream topped with raspberry purée
petit-beurre [pɔti] [bœ:r]	butter cookie
petite marmite [pɔtit] [marmit]	clear soup made with meat, poultry, marrow bones, stock pot vegetables, and cabbage; usually served with toast and sprinkled with grated cheese
petit pain [pɛ̃]	roll
pilaf [pilaf]	rice sautéed in oil and cooked with a variety of seasonings
poisson [pwasɔ̃]	fish
poivre [pwa:vr]	pepper
pomme [pɔm]	apple
porc [pɔ:r]	pork
potage [pɔta:ʒ]	soup, usually with cream base

pot-au-feu [po] [o] [fø]   French version of the boiled beef dinner

pots de crème au chocolat [ʃɔkɔla]   rich chocolate dessert

poulet [pulɛ]   chicken

poulet à la Marengo [marɛ̃go]   a method of cooking chicken by browning it in oil, adding wine, and serving it with a garnish of fried eggs, mushrooms, and crawfish

poulet chasseur [ʃasœːr]   chicken prepared with sautéed mushrooms, shallots, and white wine and tomatoes

poulet rôti a l'estragon [roti] [ɛstragɔ̃]   roast chicken with tarragon

printanière, à la [prɛ̃tanje]   garnished with a variety of spring vegetables

prix fixe [pri] [fiks]   at a set price

profiterole [prɔfitrɔl]   eclair-like pastry; may be filled with ice cream, any purée, or a custard, jam, or other sweet filling

provençale, à la [prɔvɑ̃sal]   cooked in the style of Provence, usually with tomatoes, garlic, olives, and eggplant

purée [pyre]   food that has been mashed or put through a sieve or processed in a blender

quenelles [kənɛl]   dish made with ground fish or meat blended with cream

quiche Lorraine [kiʃ]   a tart made with eggs, cream, cheese, and bacon

ragout [ragu]   a dish made from meat, poultry, or fish that has been cut up and browned; may or may not include vegetables

ratatouille [ratatuːj]   a mixture of eggplant, zucchini, squash, onions, tomatoes, and peppers; may be served hot or cold

ravigote [ravigɔt]   a white sauce, hot or cold, highly

	seasoned with thyme and coarsely ground black pepper
reine de saba [rɛn] [saba]	cake of chocolate, rum, and almonds
ris de veau [ri]	sweetbreads of veal
riz [ri]	rice
Robert [r]	sauce of onion, white wine, and mustard; served with grilled pork dishes
rognons [rɔɲɔ̃]	kidneys
saucisson [sosisɔ̃]	large sausage; sliced for serving
saumon [somɔ̃]	salmon
sec [sɛk]	dry
sel [sɛl]	salt
sorbet [sɔrbɛ]	sherbet; made from fruit or liqueurs
soufflé [sufle]	dish made with puréed ingredients, thickened with egg yolks and beaten egg whites; may be made with vegetables, fish, meat, fruit, nuts, or liqueurs; served as an appetizer, a main dish, or a dessert
specialité de la maison [spesjalite] [mezɔ̃]	specialty of a particular restaurant
steak au poivre [pwa:vr]	steak made with crushed peppercorns
steak tartare [tarta:r]	uncooked ground meat seasoned with salt and pepper and served with a raw egg yolk on top and with capers, chopped onion, and parsley on the side
sucre [sykr]	sugar
suprêmes de volaille [syprɛ:m] [vɔla:j]	chicken breasts
sur commande [kɔmɑ̃d]	made to your special order
tarte [tart]	pie
thé [té]	tea

tournedos [turnado]	small slice of beef, round and thick, from the heart of the filet of beef; sautéed or grilled
tranche [trã:ʃ]	slice
truffe [tryf]	truffle, a fungus that grows underground
truite [tryit]	trout
varié [varje]	assorted
vichyssoise [viʃiswa:z]	a cream soup of leeks, potatoes, and chicken broth; served cold
vin [vẽ]	wine
vinaigrette [vinagrɛt]	sauce of oil, mustard, and vinegar, seasoned with salt and pepper and, at times, herbs
volaille [vɔla:j]	fowl, poultry

6

CLEARING A PATH IN THE WORDS

A Word fitly spoken is like apples of gold in settings of silver.
—PROVERBS 25:11

WORD EXORCISES

Deleting weak words week by week

Adopt the modest goal of deleting two weak words per week and you will rid yourself of one hundred unwanted words in less than a year's time.

What is the cost of a word?

According to *Business Week,* the orange growers paid the raisin growers $250,000 for the privilege of using the word **Sunkist**. If you ask me, the orange growers had a bargain, for the aura that surrounds the word **Sunkist** evokes such a positive response.

But negative words are costly, too. To date, cost analysts have not put a dollars and cents figure on negative words. But the cost is there all the same and it is enormous.

To my certain knowledge, the words *ain't* and *youse* have cost quite a few jobs. I also know of turndowns as a result of pronouncing **Illinois** incorrectly and of saying the word **Realtor** * as though it had *la* in the middle instead of *al.*

---

* **Realtor**: A real-estate agent affiliated with the National Association of Real Estate Boards.

Please don't assume that a college degree—or even a graduate degree—assures you an error-free vocabulary. It doesn't. For too long we've emphasized adding words to the vocabulary. Careful and deliberate deletion of words is just as important. So is careful scrutiny and refinement of the words and phrases we intend to keep in our word storehouse. You'll notice I've included not only words for deletion but also words that require this careful scrutiny.

Some of the words in the exorcise section appear elsewhere in the book. This is deliberate. I did it for the purpose of reinforcement. Then, too, it's easy to skip certain sections of a book and miss the total message. I don't want this to happen to you.

There is no need to wait until the start of a new year to begin building a vital and vigorous vocabulary. Begin at the appropriate spot as soon as you acquire the book and don't stop until you've completed all the material.

These exorcises will be doubly effective if you will also identify and include two words each week that are your special troublemakers.

JANUARY

One kind word can warm three winter months.

—JAPANESE PROVERB

January, the first month of the year, is named for the Roman god Janus (pronounced **jay-nus**).

Although Janus is usually shown with two faces—one looking forward and the other backward—he represents the beginning of things. This is because he was the god of doors and gates in Roman mythology. People used to pray to him when they were about to begin something new.

So pray if you wish but do accompany your prayers with action; specifically, making this the year you rid yourself of verbal garbage.

January is the month of cruises. If you're lucky enough to

go on one, don't embarrass yourself by calling an **ocean liner** a **boat**. Since ships carry lifeboats, this should be an easy way to remember the correct word.

Thoughts of travel also serve as reminders to use the correct place name and to pronounce it correctly. Examples:

- It is **Algiers** (with an **s** at the end).
- It is **Tangier** (without an **s**).
- It is **The Sahara** and not **The Sahara Desert** (**Sahara** means "desert" in Arabic, so don't say *desert* twice).
- Say **Sierras** rather than the **Sierra mountains** (**Sierra**, of Spanish derivation, is inherent in *mountain* so you don't need to say *mountains* twice).

While you're at it, do remember that the **s** in **Illinois** is silent, and that **Spokane** is pronounced as though the second syllable were **can** and not *cane*.

No matter where you wander, if you wonder how the name of the place is pronounced, ask someone who knows. Usually the mayor of the town or a representative from the Chamber of Commerce can give you the acceptable pronunciation.

Exorcises

First week:	**undoubtably**	There is no such word. The word you want is **undoubt-edly**. Let's hear the **ted**.
	worsh	The word is **wash**.
Second week:	**wrench**	This word is acceptable if you're referring to a tool. It is not acceptable to say, *I'm going to* wrench *out some clothes.* The correct word here is **rinse**. Nor is it acceptable to say *heartwrenching*

		experience. The correct word is **heartrending**.
	youse	Rid yourself of this word.
Third week:	**you know**	This phrase was the biggest "nay" vote-getter in the Feeble-Phrase Finder.
	okay	When used as a conversational filler, the word **okay** is an irritant to the listener. It is particularly irritating if you use it as a question. Let's rid ourselves of it. Okay? Another equally offensive filler is **uhm**—exorcise it!
Fourth week:	**bullion**	Pronounced **bool'•yǝn**. Refers to gold or silver with regard to quantity rather than value. The word is sometimes used to refer to gold or silver bars, ingots or plates.
	bouillon	Pronounced **boo'•yon**. A clear broth.

FEBRUARY

A man cannot speak but he judges and reveals himself. With his will, or against his will, he draws his portrait to the eye of others by every word. Every opinion reacts on him who utters it.

—RALPH WALDO EMERSON

The word **February** comes from the Latin word *Februarius* which in turn comes from the word meaning "to purify." Let us work in this month of February toward the purification of our use of words.

How about starting our word purification with the word

February? It's pronounced **feb'•rōō•er•ē**. Yes, I know, Walter Cronkite has persisted in dropping the first **r**. He can get away with doing so; such a practice can be hurtful to the rest of us. While we're sounding **r**'s, it might be well to call attention to the word **library**. Let's sound both **r**'s in this word too.

Because Lent so often begins in February, this seems an appropriate time to include a couple of words that hurt the ears of ministers. The first is the word **offertory** (just four syllables—there is no **a** in the middle) and the second is **Revelation** as in the Book of Revelation (no **s** at the end of the word).

Exorcises

First week:	**theirselves**	The word is **themselves**.
	somewheres	The word is **somewhere**.
Second week:	**preventative**	**Preventive** is preferred.
	prespiration	The word is **perspiration**; the first syllable is **per** and not **pre**.
Third week:	**recognizance**	"A bond or obligation binding a person to some act such as a court appearance."
	reconnaissance	"The examination or survey of a region; The activity of reconnoitering."
Fourth week:	**reoccur**	**Recur** is preferred.
	irregardless	The correct word is **regardless**.

MARCH

The Moving Finger writes; and having writ,
Moves on: nor all thy Piety nor Wit
Shall lure it back to cancel half a Line,
Nor all thy Tears wash out a Word of it.

—Edward Fitzgerald's translation of
Omar Khayyam Edition 1 (the *Rubaiyat*)

March was the first month of the ancient Roman calendar and was called *Martius.* When Julius Ceasar revised the calendar, he moved the beginning of the year from March to January. The name **March** honors Mars, the Roman god of war.

Because March is named for the god of war, let's make war on all words and phrases that dampen the enthusiasm of others. There are killer phrases that don't produce "hear"-ache to the listening ear but that do produce an ache to the spirit of the listener. I'm thinking of phrases such as:

"You decide."

"I don't care."

"Forget it."

"No way."

"It doesn't matter."

"We've tried that before."

"I know just what you're going to say."

March is a good time to bury such conversational cripplers.

Exorcises

First week:	**pitcher**	"A container made of glass, china, silver, or other material, with a handle at one side and a lip at the other." Do not confuse with:
	picture	"A drawing, painting, portrait, or photograph." Be careful to have a **k** sound in the first syllable; it is pronounced **pik'•chər**.
Second week:	**onct**	The correct word is **once**. No **t** at the end.
	twict	The correct word is **twice**. No **t** at the end.
Third week:	**humble**	Sound the **h** at the beginning of this word.

	height	There is a **t** at the end of this word. It rhymes with kite. Learn to spell it and you won't want to put a **th** at the end.
Fourth week:	**violet**	This is the flower for March. Learn to use all three syllables in pronouncing the word.
	gen*ea*logy	Pronounced **jē•nē•äl′•ə•jē**. I'll bet if you learn to spell it, you'll also pronounce it correctly. It refers to the record of the descent of a family; lineage.

APRIL

Words are both better and worse than thoughts; they express them, and add to them; they give them power for good or evil; they start them on an endless flight, for instruction and comfort and blessing, or for injury and sorrow and ruin.

—Tryon Edwards

April, the fourth month of the year, is named for Aprilis. Aprilis is a Latin word meaning "to open." Let's designate April as the month to open—to actually clear—any clogged lines of communication.

There are soft, comforting words and phrases that can ease tensions. Learn to use them and you'll improve all your relationships.

Here are a few examples of soothing words and phrases:

• **Second mother** sounds warmer and less formal than *stepmother*. In fact, I tested the word *stepmother* in word clinics. When I asked what word, what adjective, fits the word *stepmother,* most respondents said "cruel." **Mother,** or even **second mother,** does not evoke a negative response. Adoptive mothers and fathers can be spared much pain if their children refer to their natural or birth parents in that way rather than making a distinction between "real" parents and adoptive ones. The happiest adoptive relationship I know is enhanced because the children refer to their adoptive mother as **mother** and to their late mother—whom they remember well—as their **first mother.**

- Words have a bearing on the in-law relationship too. It sounds friendlier to say, **I'd like you to meet Mary's mother,** than it does to say, *This is my mother-in-law.*
- And **I'll always remember** is more effective than *I'll never forget.*

Exorcises

First week:	**diamond**	April's birthstone is the diamond. Please make it three syllables.
	palm	Palm Sunday often arrives in April. When it does, do pronounce **palm** correctly (the **l** is sounded).
Second week:	**it don't**	**It doesn't** is correct. *It don't* is a contraction of *it do not.*
	between you and I	It is **between you and me.**
Third week:	**continue on**	continue
	start up	start
Fourth week:	**consensus of opinion**	consensus
	each and every	Use one or the other—not both.

MAY

Not in books only, nor yet in oral discourse, but often also in words there are boundless stores of moral and historic truth,

*and no less of passion and imagination laid up, from which
lessons of infinite worth may be derived.*

—RICHARD WHATELY

Believe what you choose about how May was named. Some
educators say that **May** is short for *majores,* the Latin word
for older men. These same educators say that June was considered sacred to the *juniores* or young men. I lean toward
the popular view that May was named for Maia, the Roman
goddess of spring and growth.

The most famous horse race in the United States, the Kentucky Derby, takes place on the first Saturday in May at
Churchill Downs, Louisville, Kentucky. May, then, is a good
time to polish our use of a couple of words that relate to
horses. The word **equine** ("pertaining to or characteristic of a
horse") rhymes with **mine, ē•kwīn.** And do take a good look
at the word **jodhpurs.** *You'll notice that it's* **hp** *there in the*
middle of the word and not **ph,** *so pronounce it accordingly.
Yes, say* **jod•poors.**

May is also the month in which we observe Memorial
Day. It's appropriate to mention that to call it *Decoration
Day* is not considered quite so "up-scale" or "on-top-of-it" as
to call it **Memorial Day.**

Because many students become graduates or former students in May, let's also pause to study the word **alumnus.**

Exorcises

First week:	**alumnus**	This is the masculine singular form. Say **uh•lum'•nus**
	alumni	This is the masculine plural form. It is also used to refer to a group of *men and women.* Say **uh•lum'•nī.**
	alumna	This is the feminine singular form. Say **uh•lum'•nuh.**

	alumnae	This is the feminine plural. Say **uh•lum'•nee**.
Second week:	**can**	**Can** refers to capability. For example: **I can finish this typing today.**
	may	Refers to permission or possibility. For example: **May I borrow your pen? I may need it.**
Third week:	**incidently**	The word is **incidentally**. Do notice that it has five syllables.
	bovine	If you'll remember that part of the word is **vine**, you'll probably pronounce it correctly. It is **bō•vīn** ("of or pertaining to a cow or a member of the cow family").
Fourth week	**we was**	Say **we were**.
	we done	Say **we did**.

JUNE

No man has a prosperity so high or firm, but that two or three words can dishearten it; and there is no calamity which right words will not begin to redress.

—RALPH WALDO EMERSON

Many authorities believe the Romans named June for Juno, the patron goddess of marriage. Others believe the name was taken from *juniores,* the Latin word for young men.

Since June is the month of weddings, it's fitting to give some thought to the words we use at this time. If ever "out-of-it" and "on-top-of-it" words take on importance, it's when we marry. My first awareness of this came about years ago through a discussion with a society editor. This is what she actually told me, "I can tell a lot about a family's background by the words they use in the write-up of the engage-ment or wedding. If they refer to a 'honeymoon' instead of a 'wedding trip,' or if they say, 'bride and groom' instead of 'bride and bridegroom,' I know that it [the wedding] is not a distinguished affair." When I asked if this influenced the amount of newspaper space allotted to the event, I received only a wry smile in answer.

Before you blast the society editor—or me—I should report that many cultured people agree with her assessment. Fur-ther, I should also report that many newspapers insist on the use of "wedding trip" and "bride and bridegroom" in de-scribing nuptials.

I see that I have another *flag* in my notes for the month of June. It's this reminder: The Wimbledon Championships (premier event of tennis) have passed the one hundredth anniversary, yet many sportscasters persist in pronouncing the name **Wimbledon** incorrectly. I guess the trick is to first learn to spell the word. Do notice that there is a **b** in the middle instead of a **p** and that the final syllable is **don** and not **ton**.

Exorcises

First week:	fiancé	The word has three syllables. It's **fē•än•sā′**. "A man en-gaged to be married."
	fiancée	This word has the same pro-nunciation as the masculine word **fiancé.** "A woman en-gaged to be married."
Second week:	congratulations	Do note that the word has a **t** in the middle and not a **d**. It is proper to congratulate the bridegroom but it is not proper to congratulate the bride; you may congratulate the happy couple.
	best wishes	Good wishes may be offered

to either the bride or the bridegroom.

Third week: **The Reverend Mister** (or **Doctor**) **Brown** It is not considered good form to refer to the minister as *Reverend So-and-So;* put a **the** in front of it if you're referring to him or her. If addressing him or her, use the desired designation, **Mr., Dr., Ms., Miss,** or **Mrs.**

champagne The purists insist that **champagne** comes only from Champagne (a region and former province of northeastern France). I mention it just so you'll know. The rest of us use the word to refer to sparkling white wine.

Fourth week: **candelabrum** "A large decorative candlestick." This is the singular form of the word. If you'll notice that the first part of the word is spelled **can de** (instead of *candle*) you'll say it right.

candelabra This is the plural form of the word. It means "a large candlestick having several arms or branches."

medium This is the singular form of the word. For example, **Radio is a popular medium.**

media This is the plural form of the word. For example, **The news media were here.**

JULY

The knowledge of words is the gate of scholarship.

—JOHN WILSON

July was the fifth month in the calendar of the ancient Romans. It was called *Quintilis,* meaning "fifth." When Julius Caesar, who was born in July, rearranged the calendar, he named the month for himself.

July seems to be the month of independence worldwide. Canada celebrates July 1 as Dominion Day. The United States celebrates July 4 as Independence Day; it is also celebrated as Independence Day in the Philippines. The celebration of independence takes place on July 5 in Venezuela; on July 9 in Argentina; on July 21 in Belgium; on July 25 in The Netherlands; and on July 28 in Peru. France celebrates Bastille Day on July 14.

A well-worn Martin family joke is this: One of us will say, "Do they have the fourth of July in Canada?" The second replies, "Of course not, it's a U.S. holiday." To which the first responds, "Then how do they get from the third to the fifth?"

Sorry to hand you this low-grade humor but it is *one* way to remember that the holiday is **Independence Day** and not the *fourth of July.*

July is a good time to think of words that relate to our independence. There is **government**, for example. Let's remember to sound the **n** in the middle of the word. And let's remind ourselves that the full title of the chief justice is **Chief Justice of the United States** (not *Chief Justice of the Supreme Court*).

If you happen to visit Washington, D.C., as so many do in July, do include a visit to the Smithsonian Institution. Please call it the Smithsonian **Institution** and not the Smithsonian *Institute.*

Exorcises

First week:	**cold slaw**	It is **cole slaw**; not *cold slaw*.
	sherbert	It is **sher*bet***. *The second syllable is **bet**, not bert.*
Second week	**bretzel**	There is no such word; it is **pretzel**.
	marshmellow	They may be mellow but the second part of the word is **mallow**. It is **marshm*a*llow**.
Third week:	**ek cetera**	It is not *ek cetera* but **et cetera**. Please sound the **t** in the word **et**.
	ex*pear*ament	The word is **experiment**; there is no *spear* sound in the word.
Fourth week:	**excape**	There is no such word as *excape;* the word is **escape**. Sound that **s** in the first syllable.
	enthused	**Enthusiastic** is the correct word.

AUGUST

Learn the value of a man's words and expressions, and you know him. Each man has a measure of his own for everything; this he offers you inadvertently in his words. He who has a superlative for everything wants a measure for the great or small.

—John Caspar Lavater

August was the sixth month of the year in the early Roman calendar. They called it *Sextilis,* meaning "sixth." When the Emperor Augustus renamed the month for himself, he also lengthened it to thirty-one days. In case you're wondering, he took the extra day from February.

August is a good time to take a look at words such as **drought** and **temperature** and **vegetables**. You'll notice that **drought** ends with a **t** and is therefore pronounced **drout**. The word **drouth** has also gained acceptance. Both refer to a long dry period. The word **temperature** is often used when we mean **fever**. One of my favorite talk show hosts (nationally syndicated) mentioned that "Reggie Jackson has a temperature and therefore can't play baseball today." Three people told me about it. Who knows how many called the station. Of course, Reggie has a temperature. Don't we all? And this reminds me of the doctor who was asked by an anxious wife if her husband, the patient, had blood pressure. "Yes," the doctor replied, "and it's a little low."

The preferred pronounciation of **vegetable** is **vej'•tə•bəl**, although **vej'•ət•ə•bəl** is also correct. But, please, don't use the word *veggies!*

Exorcises

First week:	**anxious**	"Uneasy because of thoughts or fears about what could happen; troubled."
	eager	"Wanting very much."
Second week:	**larnyx**	There is no such word; the word you want is **larynx**. It is pronounced **lar'•ingks**.
	temperature	Be sure to pronounce all four syllables.
Third week:	**adverse**	"Hostile; antagonistic in design or effect." **Adverse** circumstances.
	averse	"Unwilling." Careful speakers and writers make a distinction between the words **averse** and **adverse**. To be **averse** to something expresses opposition on the subject's part. That which is **adverse** to

		a person or thing denotes op-position contrary to the person's will.
Fourth week:	**regard**	"Consider, consideration; care for, respect; look at."
	regards	"Good wishes"; he sends his **regards**. One would say **in** or **with regard to** but not *in* or *with regards to.*

SEPTEMBER

Words may be either servants or masters. If the former they may safely guide us in the way of truth. If the latter they intoxicate the brain and lead into swamps of thought where there is no solid footing.

Among the sources of those innumerable calamities which from age to age have overwhelmed mankind, may be reckoned as one of the principal, the abuse of words.

—BISHOP GEORGE HORNE

September retains the name that comes from the Latin *septem,* meaning "seven." In the old Roman calendar it was the seventh month; hence the name **September** was appropriate. It became the ninth month when Julius Caesar changed the calendar.

Because Labor Day is celebrated on the first Monday of the month in Canada and the United States, it's an excellent time to review words that relate to work.

Certainly if you want to become a **Realtor,** you should know that the first part of the word is **real,** not *re·la,* and that it is usually capitalized. If you study to become an **ophthalmologist**—or if you visit one—learn that there is a **ph** in the first syllable of the word and that it gets the **f** sound. And take a good look at the word **veterinarian.** Granted it's a mouthful, but do sound all six syllables.

Even though President Eisenhower mispronounced the

word **nuclear**, that doesn't excuse the rest of us. The word is **noo′•kle•ər**: not *noo•kyoo•′ər*.

Exorcises

First week:	**manufacture**	The second syllable is **u**, not **uh**.
	periodontist	Dentists who specialize in periodontics complain that many persons omit the first **o** both in pronunciation and in spelling.
Second week:	**criterion**	This is the single form of the word; do not interchange with **criteria**, the plural form of the word.
	phenomenon	This is the singular form of the word.
	phenomena	This is the plural form.
Third week:	**prostate**	Refers to a gland.
	prostrate	Lying face down in submission or adoration or from the heat.
Fourth week:	**creek**	"A small stream of water; a brook." Do not confuse with **crick**.
	crick	The word rhymes with **sick**. It refers to a muscle spasm.

I can't resist telling you why I take delight in including **phenomenon** and **phenomena**. In promoting the first edition of *Word Watcher's Handbook,* I was a guest of Fred Griffith on Cleveland's "The Morning Exchange." I was thrown completely off-balance when an off-camera assistant scribbled a note during our interview. The note said, "Talk about the word phenomen*um*." For a couple of minutes there I thought the assistant knew something I didn't. Luckily, Mr. Griffith is truly professional. Very smoothly, he began a discussion of the words **phenomenon** and **phenomena**. Then, when he perceived that my panic had subsided, he turned to me for a discussion of the words **criteria** and **criterion**.

OCTOBER

The weaker the ideas, the stronger the language. A person whose thinking lacks substance often laces it with profanity in an effort to give it muscle. In a word—he's intellectually bankrupt.

—ANN LANDERS

Although October is the tenth month of the year, its name derives from its having been the eighth month in the Roman calendar. Attempts to change the name didn't work; the Roman senate tried to name the month *Antonius* after a Roman emperor, *Fautinus* after his wife, and *Tacitus* after a Roman emperor but the people persisted in calling it **October**.

Let's celebrate the month of October by giving the **o** sound to words that require it; words such as **piano, potato, Ohio, window,** and **fellow.**

A television station manager told me that if there hadn't been a piano near a window when he applied for his first job as an announcer, he might have been hired. You guessed it, he referred to the pian*uh* near the wind*uh.* Fortunately, he asked his interviewer why he was turned down, and, as he put it, "I haven't committed those sins since."

October is also a good time to remember that **Halloween** is a hallowed time, not a hollow one. And that **pumpkin** is pronounced **pump'•kin**. If you'll pick plump pumpkins, you'll remember that plump and pump rhyme and have no more trouble.

Exorcises

First week: **Eyetalian**   There is no such word; it is **Italian**. Think of the word

		Italy and it won't trouble you; you wouldn't say *Eyetaly.*
	ain't	Yes, I know that some dictionaries include this word, but it still hurts many ears.
Second week:	**accidently**	The word is **accidentally** and it has five syllables.
	most unique	**Unique** means "one of a kind." You don't need to qualify the word.
Third week:	**less**	**Less** means "not so much." Say **fewer** when you refer to something that can be counted. Beer that has **fewer** calories is **less** filling.
Fourth week:	**amount**	**Amount** means "aggregate." We use **amount** when we think of things in terms of bulk. **Number** refers to things you can count. The **number** of assignments was higher in his class. The **amount** of time wasted was very small.

NOVEMBER

Words are but the signs and counters of knowledge, and their currency should be strictly regulated by the capital which they represent.

—CALEB C. COLTON

In the Roman calendar, November was the ninth month; it was named for *novem,* the Latin word for nine. Tiberius Caesar refused the Roman Senate's offer to name November for him after November became the eleventh month. As he refused, he asked, "What will you do if you have thirteen emperors?" So July (for Julius Caesar) and August (for Augustus Caesar) remain the only two months named for Roman emperors.

At the top of my notes for November I have this reminder: A **turkey** is a bird, do not refer to your friends as turkeys. Also, I see this: Honor the veterans on **Veteran's Day** by pronouncing **veteran** correctly. The word has three syllables.

I don't need a reminder to think of food in connection with November. My taste buds are a-quiver at memories of Thanksgivings past and words such as **succulent** and **savory** abound. But back to the business at hand. This is a good time to remember that the **h** in **thyme** is silent, that **paté** has two syllables, that **vichyssoise** is pronounced **vish'•ē•swaź** and that **rarebit** is not rabbit. And if you can't say **Chablis** as **sha•blē**, it's best to order white wine with your turkey.

Exorcises

First week:	**culinary**	If you'll think of the word cute, you'll say this correctly. It's **kyoo'•lə•nə'r•ē.**
	cuisine	Pronounce it **kwi•zē'n.**
Second week:	**herb**	The **h** is silent.
	human	Sound the **h.**
Third week:	**quiche**	Say **kēsh.**
	kebab	Even though the second syllable is spelled **bab**, it is pronounced **bob.**
Fourth week:	**hors d'oeuvre**	Say **ôr•durv'.** The pronunciation is the same for the plural form, **hors d'oeuvres.**
	gourmet	My friend, Emilie Jacobson, included this comment in a recent letter, "I still remember Ogden Nash, a *great* purist, sitting in my office growling, '**Gourmet** is not an adjective.' " Let's re-

member that the word is
a noun and that it's pro-
nounced **goŏr•mā'**.

DECEMBER

There are words which sever hearts more than sharp swords;
there are words the point of which sting the heart through the
course of a whole life.

— FREDERIKA BREMER

December, the twelfth and last month of our calendar year,
was so named because it was originally the tenth month of
the year in the ancient Roman calendar. *Decem* means "ten"
in Latin.

If you live in Zinzinnati—woops, I mean Cincinnati—you'll
understand my warning about putting a z in the word **December**. Those of us with German or Dutch background tend
to introduce a **z** sound every chance we get. The **z** sound in
the second syllable of **December** must irritate a great many
ears for I've received a number of notes about it. The **s** sound
in the word **sink** has also incurred a few complaints. One
person took the trouble to explain, "In the old days sinks
were made of zinc, maybe that's why people still say *zink*
when they mean **sink**. Anyway, put a stop to it, will you?" I'll
try.

Another of my December reminders has a sketch of Santa
Claus pointing to the North Pole. Underneath the sketch I've
written, "talk about **arctic**." I believe that is to remind me to
remind you that the word **arctic** has two **c**'s and both are
sounded.

There is also a note about **Hanukkah**, the Jewish Feast of
Lights or Feast of Dedication. The word is usually pro-
nounced **Hah'•noo•kah** (spellings vary; it is Hanukkah,
Hanukah, or Chanukah).

And there is this reminder: Many Christians are pained by
the use of the word *Xmas* for **Christmas.** I'll pass along this

comment, "The fact that **x** is often used to represent the unknown factor or quantity is no comfort."

Exorcises

First week:	poinsettia	It is pronounced **poin•sĕt•ē′•ə**. The flower/shrub is named for J. R. Poinsett, a minister to Mexico.
	fiscal	"Of or pertaining to finances." Do note that the word has just two syllables.
Second week:	Calvary	Place near Jerusalem where Christ was crucified. I always remember the distinction between **Calvary** and **cavalry** by associating **Calvin** (the great Christian) with **Calvary** and the word **cavalier** (which comes from the word **horseman**) with **cavalry**. The sequence of letters does it for me.
	cavalry	Has to do with horses. See above.
Third week:	can't hardly	*Can't hardly* is a double negative and should be avoided. Say **can hardly**.
	giblet	It is pronounced **jib′•let.**
Fourth week:	grievous	Say **grē′•vus**. Causing grief.
	suspicion	You have a **suspicion**; you **suspect**. Do not say, "I suspicion."
Bonus word:	decimate	This is from the Latin *decem* (ten). It means, literally, to "select by lot and kill one in every ten." Many persons (nonpurists) use it to mean "kill or destroy a large number."

BIBLIOGRAPHY

The American Heritage Dictionary of the English Language. New York: American Heritage Publishing Company, Inc., 1973.

Bates, Jefferson D. *Writing With Precision.* Washington, D.C.: Acropolis Books Ltd., 1978.

Bernstein, Theodore M. *The Careful Writer, A Guide to English Usage.* New York: Atheneum, 1967.

Bernstein, Theodore M. *Reverse Dictionary.* New York: Quadrangle/The New York Times Book Company, 1975.

Flesch, Rudolph. *Say What You Mean.* New York: Harper & Row Publishers, Inc., 1972.

Fowler, H.W. *A Dictionary of Modern English Usage.* Kingsport, Tennessee: Oxford University Press, 1944.

Martin, Phyllis. *Martin's Magic Formula for Getting the Right Job.* New York: St. Martin's Press, 1981.

The New Dictionary of Thoughts. New York: Standard Book Company, 1956.

Newman, Edwin. *A Civil Tongue.* New York: Warner Books, 1977.

Newman, Edwin. *Strictly Speaking.* New York: Warner Books, 1974.

Safire, William. *On Language.* New York: Times Books, 1980.

Stewart, Marjabelle Young and Marian Faux. *Executive Etiquette.* New York: St. Martin's Press, 1979.

Strunk, William Jr. and E. B. White. *The Elements of Style,* Second Edition. New York: Macmillan Publishing Company, Inc., 1972.

The World Book Encyclopedia. Chicago: Field Enterprises Educational Corporation, 1960.

ORDER INFORMATION

I welcome your comments about the second edition of *Word Watcher's Handbook*. Do bear in mind that I intend to provoke thought, not outrage, with this book. I'm *reporting* on what hurts listeners' ears. I do not say that everything I've included here hurts my ears. Nor do I say I'm free of all the "hear"-ache I talk about.

Those who wrote in response to my request for comments last time taught me that I have a lot to learn. For example, I learned that the quotation is "a Parthian shot" and not "a parting shot." I also learned that a "lion's share" means all of it, not most of it as I thought. Lions don't share.

Now a Word from You, Please

Phyllis Martin:

How about _____?

And shouldn't _____ be _____?

Suggestion for your next edition _____

_____

Signed: (if you wish) _____

Student _____   Education _____   Age: under 21 _____

Occupation _____   Sex _____   21 + _____

Order Form

Extra copies of *Word Watcher's Handbook* may be ordered directly from the publisher.

If you found this book useful, you might also be interested in *Martin's Magic Formula for Getting the Right Job,* a practical and result-oriented guide to job hunting. Both books may be ordered by writing:

St. Martin's Press, 175 Fifth Avenue, New York, N.Y. 10010. Please make check or money order payable to St. Martin's Press.

- -

Please send _____ copies of *Word Watcher's Handbook* @ 4.95 plus postage and handling charges of 75¢ for the first book and 35¢ for each additional book, to:

Name_____

Address_____

City_____ State_____ Zip_____

- -

Please send _____ copies of *Martin's Magic Formula for Getting the Right Job* @ $5.95 plus postage and handling charges of 75¢ for the first book and 35¢ for each additional book, to:

Name_____

Address_____

City_____ State_____ Zip_____

- -

INDEX

October, 117–118
"offertory," pronunciation of, 104
"Ohio," pronunciation of, 117
"okay," 103
Omar Khayyam, 104
"onct," for "once," 105
"On-top-of-it" words, 76–80, 109
"ophthalmologist," pronunciation of, 115
"Out-of-it" words, 76–80, 109

Packard, Vance, 75
"palm," pronunciation of, 107
partial/partly, 56
"paté," pronunciation of, 119
"periodontist," pronunciation of, 116
persecute/prosecute, 56
"phenomenon" vs. "phenomena," 116–117
"piano," pronunciation of, 117
pitch, of voice, 4
"pitcher," for "picture," 1, 105
place names, 102
"plus and minus words," 76, 81
"poinsettia," pronunciation of, 121
political words, 76
positive listeners, 5
positive words, value of, 100
"potato," pronunciation of, 117
"prespiration," for "perspiration," 104
"preventative," for "preventive," 104
"prioritize," 6
Procter & Gamble, 20
professional jargon, 18–19
pronunciation, 58–74
  flash cards for, 3, 9, 58–59
  guide to, 58–59
  of new words, 4
  recording words for, 3, 58
pronunciation key, 59
prostate/prostrate, 56, 116
"pumpkin," pronunciation of, 117
purposefully/purposely, 56

"quiche," pronunciation of, 119

ravage/ravish, 56
reading, 4
"Realtor," 100, 115
"recognizance," 104
"reconnaissance," 104
"regard," 115
"regards," 115
regime/regimen, 56
regretfully/regrettably, 56
rend/render, 56
"reoccur," for "recur," 104
"Revelation," pronunciation of, 104

Safire, William, 76
Sahara, The, 102
"second mother," response evoked by, 106–107
sensual/sexual, 56
September, 115–117
"sherbert," for "sherbet," 113
Sierras, 102
"sink," pronunciation of, 120
Smithsonian Institution, 112
snob words, 75
"somewheres," for "somewhere," 104
Spokane, pronunciation of, 102
"start up," for "start," 107
Status Seekers, The (Packard), 75
"stepmother," negative response to, 106–107
Stewart, Marjabelle Young, 86
students, xi
"Sunkist," 100
"suspicion," 121

tack/tact, 56
talking down, 34
talk shows, 4
Tangier, 102
tape recorders:
  correcting pronunciation with, 3, 58
  listening to self on, 4
"temperature," pronunciation of, 114